Route 66

The Empires of Amusement

ROSSI'S BALL ROOM

ROUTE 66 - BRAIDWOOD

SUNDAY NIGHT, JULY 14

AMATEUR NIGHT

Admission: Ladies' 10c; Gent's 25c; No other charge

DANCING EVERY SUNDAY NIGHT

Lang
THOMPSON
AND
HIS
ORCHESTRA

Route 66

The Empires of Amusement

by

THOMAS ARTHUR REPP

MOCK TURTLE PRESS: LYNNWOOD, WASHINGTON

The publisher wishes to thank the Will Rogers Heritage Trust for permission to
reprint from *Daily Telegrams: Volume III, Hoover Years, 1931–1933*
by Will Rogers, © 1981 by Oklahoma State University Press;
and Charlotte Rittenhouse for permission to reprint from
A Guide Book to Highway 66 by Jack D. Rittenhouse,
© 1946, 1989 by Jack D. Rittenhouse.

Frontispiece: Rossi's Ballroom advertising poster,
courtesy Mary Ogg.

Contents page: Meramec Caverns brochure, author's collection;
Fun Fair matchbook, courtesy Pat Thone; Fairyland Pass, courtesy Georgia Miller;
Mule Trading Post business card, courtesy Herb Baden.

Design by Thomas Arthur Repp
Jacket design by Ashley Anne Bogle

Publisher's Cataloging-in-Publication Data
(Provided by Quality Books, Inc.)

Repp, Thomas Arthur,
Route 66 : the empires of amusement / Thomas Arthur Repp. -- 1st ed.
p. cm.
Includes bibliographical references and index.
LCCN: 98-96936
ISBN: 0-9669148-0-5

1. United States Highway 66--History.
2. United States Highway 66--Description and travel.
3. Amusements--United States.
4. Automobile travel--United States. I. Title

HE356.U55R47 1999
388.1'0973   QBI98-990014

08 07 06 05 04 03 02 01 00 99   5 4 3 2 1

For Aleene Kay Albro and Zelta Davis
Herb Baden, Billie Henderson and Wanda Queenan
and all the other impresarios along Route 66
who befriended and entertained us
so well and so long.

Contents

Top: Cream City would have been a crackerjack Route 66 attraction—if it had survived. The Lyons, Ill., amusement park opened, burned and closed in the early 1900s. The park's entrance towers stood for decades afterward. Locals used them after the stock market crash of 1929—to leap to their deaths. Bottom: The opportunity to pose for a picture with animals was a Route 66 draw. Photographers understood animal appeal almost from the moment cameras were invented. In the early 1920s, this photograph was taken by a man who traveled with a goat. He knocked on doors in Detroit and enticed mothers to round up their children for a photographic keepsake.

Introduction:
The Empires of Amusement

The ringmaster has returned to Route 66. Only those spectators with ears perked and waiting heard his second coming—a kind of soft-shoe sashay over a pavement of peanut shells. Early reports say his spats are still shiny—although sticky with ice cream stains. His top hat looks crisp, and his collar appears fluffy with fresh ostrich feathers. This is no small trick after 70 years of service.

His, after all, was once the world's greatest traveling show: the extravaganza that was the roadside attraction on Route 66.

U.S. Highway 66, of course, has been riding a two-lane revival for a wild and wonderful decade. The path of pavement that lay between Chicago and Los Angeles has not only reclaimed its rank as America's favorite road, but has gained new ground as the darling thoroughfare of an autobahn-weary world. As it did more than half a century ago, Route 66 today attracts an army of artists and authors. Over the past few years, their skills have showered us with Route 66 recipes, Route 66 travelogues, Route 66 paintings and Route 66 postcards. The road lies forever enshrined as the weeping ribbon that carried the Okies west and a Corvette lover's lane through which one might cruise after Buzz and Tod.

Route 66, in fact, has of late been enshrined as just about everything but the avenue that brought us the likes of E. Mike Allred's Supernatural Raccoons.

The fact that the route's circus side has not been extensively explored in recent years has drawn little ire from the road's old tourist attraction operators. Contrariwise, these impresarios seem accustomed to waiting in line. On or off Route 66, historians have paid slim attention to curbside institutions like the show cave, the reptile house or the prairie dog village. Admittedly, these are not places that attracted Norman Rockwell or Holly Hobbie. The term, tourist trap—first put into print in 1939 by English novelist Graham Greene—probably did originate on Route 66. Odds say the expression was coined by someone's irate Uncle Ernie, angry at being pinched into an auto's back seat before the dawn of orthopedic pillows. Whatever its origin, the phrase has done lasting damage. Somehow, it suggests, all roadside attractions are cheap tricks, shell games proffered by money-hungry Pinocchios, plastic oases suffering uniformly from problems of quality and conscience.

No myth has done more to harm a greater group of people along Route 66.

In truth, most of the early Route 66 roadside attractions were Mom-and-Pop operations. They were businesses run by husbands and wives and extended families, and they were businesses fiercely concerned with customer satisfaction. By their very nature they were capsules of ingenuity that allowed individual talents to shine. Anyone could run a cafe, a service station or a motel. But it took inspiration to bury stunt men alive, run gas lines to perpetually-burning covered wagons or fix flea markets with shacks that looked like Howard Johnson's restaurants. Necessity stopped motorists for food, fuel and sleep. The operators of roadside entertainments lived by brains alone.

And by brains do some of them survive to this day. As more and more roadies take to Route 66, more and more roadies discover that the old highway offers more than classic motels and cafes. Today's Route 66 still offers places at which one can find old-fashioned fun. The people who head such establishments are a uniquely determined bunch. Many are descendants of brave souls who painted wagons bright and embarked with a whip and a postcard rack to tame the earliest alignment of the highway. These are folks who as children awoke mornings to chores of sweeping out snake pits or hammering native stones into beautiful, sellable bits; whacking loose nails back into roller coasters or hawking handmade baskets in the shadows of piano-playing chickens.

They are the last of the road's unsung heroes.

Stop and talk with them, and you'll hear of family sagas that are inseparable from the rise of the great American amusement industry. Most modern motorists don't realize this country's taste for structured diversion was a taste acquired. Time was—hardly a century and a half ago—when doctor's prescribed the proper suit to be worn while ocean swimming. Industrialization and urbanization had lifted some of the burden from the average back, and workers were learning to enjoy their new leisure time. Early resorts and a few circus-type shows sprang to their aid. But distraction didn't make a national splash until Phineas Taylor Barnum opened his American Museum in 1841.

Today, Barnum's name remains synonymous with the circus. Long before he sold his soul to saw-dust, Barnum founded the world's first roadside attraction when he opened his American Museum at the corner of Broadway and Ann Streets in New York City. Under the watch of a critical Christian eye, museums had long slipped the public a modicum of titillation through lectures, pickled beasts and other tidbits scientific. But when Barnum overhauled the failing Scudder's American Museum, he made his aim outright entertainment. Barnum filled his museum with a chorus of human "curiosities." He displayed living white whales in wake of the book *Moby Dick*. He paid a band to attract passing ears and draped his museum's facade with large, flamboyant banners.

Barnum's brand of over-the-top promotion became the model by which American amusements were made. When this country's first major world's fair—the Centennial Exhibition—came to Philadelphia in 1876, the showmen were there,

selling eccentric diversions on the outskirts of the fair. By 1895, the universe had recreated itself as Coney Island. There, in time for Independence Day, steamboat captain and daredevil Paul Boyton opened the world's first self-enclosed amusement park. Sea Lion Park was a modest enterprise, consisting of a Shoot the Chutes, an old mill ride, a lagoon and 40 trained seals. But Boyton's concept of a self-enclosed park drew the attention of more ambitious eyes. Between 1897 and 1904 the world's first great amusement parks—Steeplechase, Luna Park and Dreamland—arose on Coney Island.

The intense, international attention given these early parks is something Disneyland has never known. The first premature baby incubators to operate in the United States operated not at a hospital, but inside Dreamland Park. Sigmund Freud strolled Dreamland to study the mind's need for amusement. So popular did Steeplechase, Luna Park and Dreamland grow, that they beget bouncing baby amusement parks nationwide. These, in turn, gave rise to the carnival—a more participatory brother of the circus—which spread entertainment through towns too small to support their own amusement parks. As auto travel grew popular, and highways like Route 66 linked the land, carnival and circus workers, trick riders, stunt flyers and midway game concessionaires began to settle onto curbs across America—and into roadside attractions.

Route 66 stretched from Chicago to Los Angeles, but the amusement industry's connection to the road saw its strongest roots in the eastern half of the great highway. The sections of Arizona and New Mexico through which Route 66 sliced were, for the most part, marginally populated. Roadside attractions arose in these states, but they commonly sprouted from legitimate off-reservation trading posts that turned to tourists as their relationships with Indians grew less interdependent. In the East, roadside entertainments were as a rule built earlier and with nothing but amusement in mind. The word "park" itself proliferated among eastern attractions. Like the dance halls that freckled Route 66 in rural Illinois, many entertainments on the eastern half of the highway served locals as well as tourists. This fact alone demanded eastern playpens keep themselves well-polished and turned the largest of them into bona fide Empires of Amusement.

A smattering of those empires that gained fame along Route 66 significantly predated the highway. By 1926—the year in which Route 66 was born—the Ozarks region of Missouri was firmly established as a vacationer's paradise. Early show caves like Onondaga, King and Crystal caves had for decades welcomed visitors who arrived by train or surrey. The larger eastern cities—including Tulsa, Oklahoma, and Joplin, Missouri, had long sustained amusement parks. In Springfield, Illinois, Lincoln's Home welcomed significant numbers of visitors by 1905.

Some of the earliest eastern attractions were started by accident. The Talking Crow at the Log Cabin Inn was a personal pet that proved its worth as a drawing card after it was housed near the highway. Ozark Rock Curios and Mullen's 66 Rock Shop were founded by miners with no concrete plans to start marketing minerals. As decades passed, the roadside attraction came of age on Route 66. Aleene and Russell Kay built their Buffalo Ranch near Afton, Oklahoma, only after studying traffic patterns on four highways. Prairie Dog Town of Amarillo, Texas, was designed by a civic promoter who long calculated the best place to start an attraction to serve his city.

The Golden Age of the Route 66 Attraction followed World War II and continued through the 1950s. During this time, roadside attractions were often encountered as extensions of "essential" curbside business. Gas stations and hotels incorporated enticements to distinguish themselves from their competitors. The rise of the reptile garden—and its coiling cousin, the snake pit—was one of the period's most interesting phenomenons. But even as the cobra became curbside king, bigger and blander interstates were systematically bypassing sections of Route 66. By the end of 1985, Route 66 itself had been decertified, and the road's tourist attractions lay devastated. Aging cafes could continue to cram local mouths—and motels tiptoe forward tucking in long-term lodgers—but the roadside attraction had no substitute for the cross-country traveler.

The establishments featured in the following 34 chapters are meant to represent a cross section of those amusements that found the most fame along Route 66, those that have been all but forgotten and those that have somehow managed to survive. In each case, they are amusements selected from the eastern half, or the circus side, of the great highway. In every instance, the goal has been to record the histories of these classic curbside stops while the owners and operators themselves—or their sons, daughters, nieces and nephews—are still able to relate them.

Hopefully, these tales will inspire motorists to seek out all of the amusement empires featured—whether those establishments remain today alive and well and in brightly-colored business, or abandoned and dwindled like parts of a carousel whinnying their way into a caramel sunset.

"I used to take it as an offensive thing when people called us a tourist trap," says Route 66 historian, Davy Delgado. "It wasn't until I saw this same face a few times during the year that I thought, Hey, this guy was calling us a tourist trap. What's he doing back here? I met the same man years later, and I said, 'You're the guy who used to call us a tourist trap. Now, how many times have you been back?' And he said, 'I know, that's what I mean. I enjoy myself so much, I keep coming back here.'"

We never grow up. Of this, the divorce rate remains solid proof. But between the stones and arrows life slings, the wise participant buys a bag of peanuts. Spacious fun can still be found under the big top—and in the backseat of any automobile barreling down old Route 66. Buckle yourself in. Play with the ashtrays. Motor on toward E. Mike Allred's Supernatural Raccoons. Your driver is a dandy with ice cream on his spats, an aging ringmaster who consigns his rabbit-lined gloves to his pocket and puts his well-heeled foot forward into fabulous flavors of spumoni, rocky road and wonderfully high wire.

Long live the Route 66 circus.
Strike up the piano-playing chickens.
And get your tickets here.

FAIRYLAND PARK -- 40th Street at Harlem Ave. - LYONS, ILL.

Top: A postcard view of Fairyland shows the park's venerable carousel—pieces of which survive to this day.
Bottom: Al Miller's fire engine, available for rent and guaranteed to heat up political rallies and county fairs.

Fairyland Park & the Whoopee Coaster

s cars bumped their way west from downtown Chicago, the first sizeable tourist attraction they encountered along Route 66 was a good old-fashioned amusement park. Amusement parks, in fact, once blinked brightly near both ends of the great highway. Fairyland Park of Lyons, Illinois, had its midway mirror in the chutes and ladders of Santa Monica's Pleasure Pier. Both parks were substantially smaller than—and out-lived—nearby, bigger-wheeled brothers. Both were stitched mercifully to the outskirts of swelling cities like screwy and oily IVs. In a day before Disney-mania made mousy themes a must, neither park claimed to be anything more than a collection of rifle ranges and Tilt-A-Whirls. Both swallowed their customers without excessive fanfare—and spat them out smiling balloons.

On the west side of Harlem Avenue in Lyons, Illinois—precisely between 39th and 40th Streets—the roots of amusement reach deeper than Fairyland Park itself. The ground over which a winking wonderland would rise first served as home to a band of Romany people.

"The corner of Pershing and Harlem was—for years—a Gypsy camp," says local long-timer Louis Stastny. "When I was young, my dad consistently threatened to turn me over to the Gypsy King if I didn't behave, so I stayed in line."

Weekends saw Lyons locals visiting the Gypsy camp to find their fortunes in tea leaves, open palms and crystal balls. After nightfall, violins slit the air under crackle of campfires, and exotic aromas tickled the nose. On Sunday afternoons, one of the Romany men appeared at nearby Cermak Park leading a muzzled black bear. He'd strap roller

The Lyons Gypsy Camp served as home to the Stanley tribe of Gypsies for more than 19 years. Fortune tellers at the camp preferred payment in lace tablecloths or hand-crocheted bed spreads.

The Whoopee Coaster was one of the first amusements built specifically to snag traffic along Route 66. Locals loved it, too. "The boys in the neighborhood would sneak their bikes on it," says Gladys Yirsa. "You'd see the kids on the corner, at the show or even in Sunday school, and they'd all be bragging, 'I rode the Whoopee Coaster.' The man who ran the Whoopee spent a good deal of his time chasing kids off the thing, although, I dare say, he chased them with a smile on his face."

skates on the grizzly and let time—and a hat—pass slowly. His pet performed on a concrete square located east of the park's Ogden Avenue entrance.

The area's first formal amusement arose in the later 1920s and stretched along Lawndale Avenue and Route 66, between Lyons and McCook. The Whoopee Coaster was a one-of-a-kind carnival ride designed for the motoring public—a roller coaster made of planks and modest hills that wound around an otherwise empty field. The Whoopee Coaster offered one unique twist: Riders rode its back in their own automobiles.

"No one remembers who owned the Whoopee Coaster," says Lyons historian, Gladys Yirsa. "Every time my family went to ride the Whoopee, we saw this same old man in floppy pants and ragged shirt. He looked like he lived on the property, although I'm quite certain he didn't.

"He had a chain across the gate. You paid your admission and lined up to take your turn riding this hilly, wooden track. The old man let one car in at a time, and that car had to reach a certain point on the Whoopee Coaster before he'd let in another.

"The whole thing was made out of boards, and the railing around it wouldn't hold in any car. My dad always drove when we rode the Whoopee. My mother would be fretting, 'Be careful! Be careful!' And we kids in the back seat would be screaming, 'Go faster! Go faster!'"

By 1938, the Whoopee Coaster was kaput—done in, believe its old neighbors, by the weight of newer cars. The Gypsies had left Lyons, and local residents Richard and Helen Miller were raising the smiling steel skeletons of Fairyland Park on the old camp property.

For years, Richard's brother Charles operated Miller Amusements out of La Grange, Illinois. The company managed traveling carnivals—and provided entertainment at special events in rural Illinois. Fairyland may have been the family's first stationary endeavor, but the attractions that filled its insides were tried and true movers and shakers. Opening day enticements included a gaggle of miniature gas autos, outdoor bowling, a Ferris wheel and the attraction that would consistently top the kiddie I-gotta-go list—live pony rides.

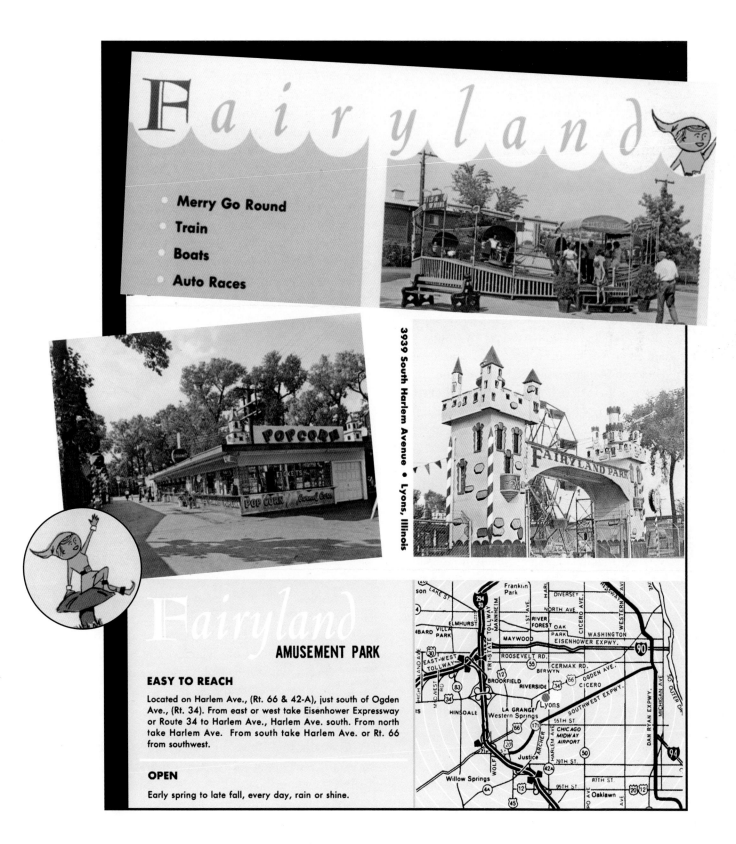

Fairyland

- Merry Go Round
- Train
- Boats
- Auto Races

3939 South Harlem Avenue • Lyons, Illinois

FAIRYLAND PARK

Fairyland
AMUSEMENT PARK

EASY TO REACH

Located on Harlem Ave., (Rt. 66 & 42-A), just south of Ogden Ave., (Rt. 34). From east or west take Eisenhower Expressway or Route 34 to Harlem Ave., Harlem Ave. south. From north take Harlem Ave. From south take Harlem Ave. or Rt. 66 from southwest.

OPEN

Early spring to late fall, every day, rain or shine.

Fairyland Park brochure features Fairyland's namesake pixies and the dream castle that stood at park's entrance. Some of the castle's stained glass windows may today be seen at the Lyons Historical Museum inside the Lyons Hofmann Tower.

"They were Shetland ponies," says Louis Stastny. "You'd climb into the saddle and an older—say 16-year-old—kid would lead you around a corral. The ponies were very popular. At that time, there were only three houses on the block. The rest was farmland. I'd ride my own horse over to Fairyland just so I could ride a pony."

Fairyland Park well-survived its first decade and the horror show of World War II. The 5-acre park with an additional 2 1/2-acre parking area seemed perfectly sized for post-war tastes as Chicagoans began to shun large city parks in favor of smaller, suburban amusement centers. Fairyland Park hired its help from the inside out, and friends and family members kept carousels and concession stands smoothly cranking. In 1955, Richard and Helen's son, Allen, and their daughter-in-law, Georgia, assumed control of the park. Soon many attractions were enclosed in a large, heated building, and Fairyland's namesake pixies thumbed tiny, tinkerbell noses at any sign of rain.

"We opened every day at one o'clock, and closed at ten or eleven," Georgia Miller says of the mechanical summer grind. "Generally, we started our season on Palm Sunday, and closed on Halloween. When Al and I took over, rides cost 12 for a dollar. We later had to raise the price to eight for a dollar."

Al Miller found an antique fire engine for sale in Tennessee. He brought the truck to Fairyland where it became a favorite attraction. Kids clamored aboard the engine's back for slow, screaming rides through the park. Drivers whipped the siren into a frenzy while a blinding flasher splashed crimson through the trees. When the engine wasn't making a spectacle of itself at Fairyland proper, it was ringing its way through small town parades and picnics—on lease from Al—with the renter's advertisement riding high in the rear.

In best barker tradition, Fairyland's own advertising traveled mostly by word of mouth. On occasion, courtesy passes appeared on neighborhood lunch counters, but advertisements in the larger Chicago papers were never to be. Despite the park's slow media dance, Fairyland far outlasted Chicago's larger parks and the coming crunch of urbanization. Chicago's Riverview Amusement Park closed in 1967, and the south side's crippled White City chuckled its last in the later 1930s. Fairyland remained airborne—boxed in by drugstores and motels—through 1977.

"Fairyland was never much trouble," Georgia Miller insists. "We had the usual small problems—kids hopping on and off the carousel or trying to sneak into the park. The only crime I remember happened one day at our novelty stand. We had a novelty stand where we sold balloons and airplanes and fireman hats, and, one day, while my sister was tending it, a lady stole a little fur monkey. But that worked out okay, too, because my sister chased her, and we did get our monkey back. We're Bohemians, you know, so no one got away with anything.

"We had a lot of loyal customers from Chicago and Berwyn, Stickney and Riverside. And we had some very beautiful rides. Our merry-go-round was purchased from White City when that park went out of business. I believe it was made by Mangels. All the horses were hand-carved."

Today, the plot over which Fairyland Park once gleamed has lost its otherworldly charm—giving way to the chunky dullness of department stores and automobile dealerships. But northwest of Fairyland's long-lost twinkle—the old merry-go-round survives after a fashion. Sold to the Barn of Barrington Restaurant in Barrington, Illinois, the carousel was disassembled and its trusty steeds set out to pasture in a Carousel Bar and Cafe. There, a seat on their whittled backs can still be had by riders eager to trot toward days gone by. Seen from their saddles, the old road west has lost precious little wonder. Turns still smell of sweetly salted peanuts; tires wheel like Tilt-A-Whirls, and Route 66—as it tumbles toward the Pacific—unwinds once again as the world's greatest traveling show.

And in the reflection of long funhouse mirrors, a fire engine happily screams.

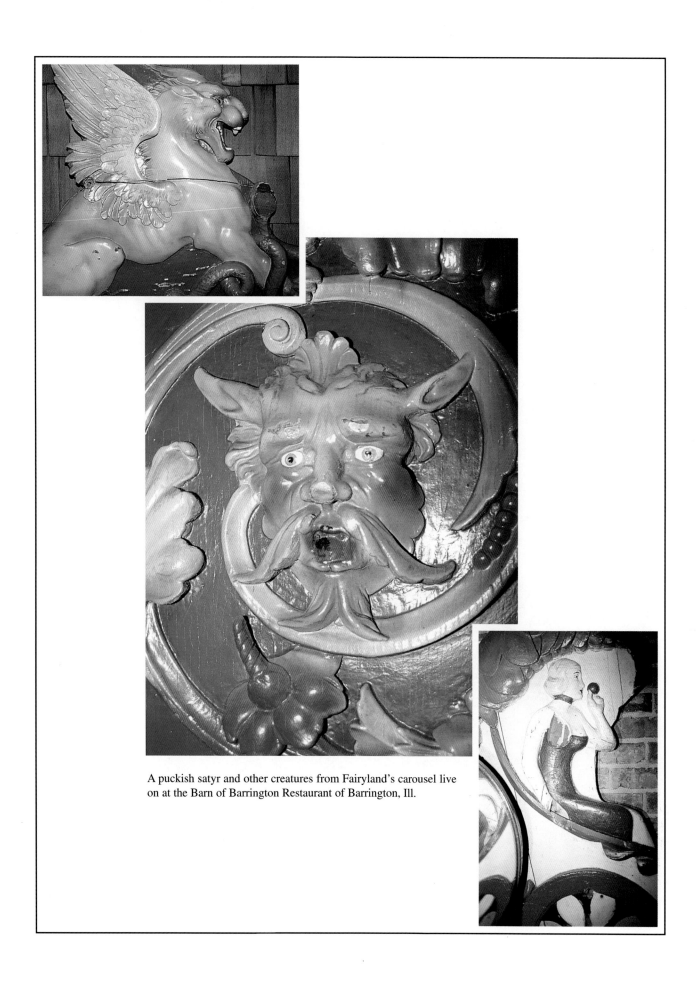

A puckish satyr and other creatures from Fairyland's carousel live on at the Barn of Barrington Restaurant of Barrington, Ill.

Pachyderm friend with Montana Charlie Reid at Montana Charlie's Little America.

Montana Charlie's Little America

If you shoot 'em in the spring,
they'll never bother you in the fall
 —Montana Charlie Reid

 icking up ink and whipping out yard-sticks, mapmakers might argue the state of Montana rests nowhere near Route 66. Montana Charlie Reid would tell such sticklers to shut up and sit on their compass points.

The sandy, dandy Chicagoan with the crisply-creased Stetson forever shading his brow never let anyone tell him how to run his show. To Montana Charlie, business was a butte where buffalo roamed, an open range of ideas and shots in the dark that burst booming and spectacular before a boggle-eyed audience. Participants received points for trick-riding. Losers slunk away under saddles of shame.

Like the bulk of baby critters, Charlie's rise to fame began in tiny, toddling steps. He was born January 22, 1895, on Chicago's Courtland Avenue. Charlie's parents managed a cannery, and they may have hoped their son would take up their tinny trade. But before adulthood could hogtie him, Charlie rode west to embrace the big sky of Browning, Montana. He lived the American Cowboy Dream, driving cattle and adopting a western style of dress that would suit him his entire life. His entry into the world of the Sells-Floto Circus was not long in following and occasioned by a man named Otto Christensen.

"Otto Christensen was a famous horse trainer," explains Charlie's son, Chuck. "He trained Liberty Horses—teams of eight or ten white horses that worked in unison. My father was struck by these performing horses, and he knew Otto Christensen well. That, I believe, inspired him to join the circus."

Trading his spurs for steam whistles, Charlie became the calliope player for the Sells-Floto Circus. He tumbled into town in wake of the Bode Wagon Company's 1906 elephant tableau band-wagon and with a company of clowns that included German-born comedy rider Otto Griebling.

Charlie developed a deep respect for these funny men. Years later, after he had grown into a truck stop king, portraits of bulb-nosed buffoons would splatter his walls. Indeed, Charlie would adopt their gregarious manner in putting on his own public face.

When Charlie returned to Chicago, he took a job with the Wells Petroleum Company. He served as secretary and chauffeur to company head, Colonel Wells. Charlie's proximity to the big man in black gave him an oily leg up. Hard work took him higher. One day, Charlie found he owned the company. As a sideline to his petroleum empire, Charlie created Refiners Pride Distributing Corporation. Both businesses sprouted gas stations as easily as magicians produce crepe-paper bouquets.

Charlie never pistol-whipped his personality into an oil magnate's mold. The playful head of his circus past first reared at Refiners Pride headquarters in Forest Park, Illinois. There an immense, empty lot abutted the company offices. Charlie decided to spruce up the property for the neighborhood birds. He covered the lot with trees and seed feeders, cookie-cut shrubbery and 1,000 tulips that, as a matter of course, would be dug up and replaced every year. Charlie christened his flowering sanctuary Montana Charlie's Bird Haven.

Trash containers at Refiners Pride gas stations grew elephant heads. The plastic pachyderms sported wide-open mouths that encouraged disposal and delighted kids.

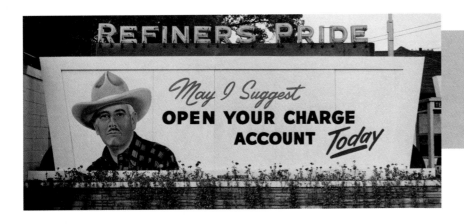

Gas station sign adjacent to the Refiners Pride Corp. offices.

On Saturdays, folks filling up at one of Charlie's Forest Park stations frequently found Charlie waiting to greet them. Toting a small basket, the Chicago cowboy approached cars and doled out free cookies and coffee cake. "He did a lot of that," remembers Charlie's son, Chuck. "At his stations he'd hang signs that read, 'Getting By Giving Is How We Built Our Business.'"

When Charlie wasn't wooing patrons at the pump, he was tipping his ten-gallon at one of his Welco Truck Stops. Charlie owned two of the diesel islands—one in Walkerton, Indiana, and one on Route 66 north of Joliet, Illinois. Both were affiliated with Wells Petroleum. The Welco Truck Stop on Route 66—painted plum and lemon yellow with wavy wood trim tracing windows like the trim on a circus wagon—grew famous for its ambitious, sideshow perks. Inside, a cubbyhole housed a barber. Sleeping rooms rested truckers. On the roof, a herd of heavy, plastic black-angus bulls silently mooed.

Charlie continued to embrace his earliest cowboy roots. In 1939, he returned to Montana to found the Burnt Leather Ranch. From that year forward, he split his time between Chicago and big sky country.

Charlie planned his last enterprise in the middle 1960s. Along Route 66, and immediately south of his Welco Truck Stop, he patched together pieces of land and began outlining the latitudes and longitudes of Montana Charlie's Little America.

On the books, Little America was built as an eccentric flea market. Behind the scenes, Charlie found he finally had his hands on an enterprise that yielded itself completely to his over-the-big-top tastes. He conceived Little America as a type of curio country, complete with drive-thru signs that welcomed bargain hunters to "Frontier Trail" and "Indian Trail." Large plastic chickens faced-off at market's middle. Candy-colored sheds housed vendors and carried names like "Miner's Supplies" and "Justice of the Peace."

Over the years the school of sheds sported many inspired paint jobs. The most unique coating occurred when Charlie took notice of reigning restaurant chain, Howard Johnson's.

"Apparently, Charlie liked the Howard Johnson's colors," says long-time Little America manager, June Walker. "He had the flea market roofs all roofed in orange with turquoise trim. For some time, this place looked like a town made up of Howard Johnson's Restaurants."

At the rear of Little America, Charlie concocted a poor cousin to his Bird Haven. The Little America Duck Pond was meant to be a pleasant diversion. Stocked each year with a flock of waddlers, the pond boasted a formal Duck House that sheltered quacks in foul weather. Unfortunately, the concentration of game birds attracted unwanted attention. The Little America Duck Pond was poached, pilfered and roasted to extinction.

Other rainy-day incidents did little lasting damage. On one occasion, a small boy too quickly employed the brake on the market's windmill. The contraption's slats snapped free and sliced earthward with the sharpness of guillotines. No one was injured. On another morning, June Walker arrived at Little America to find the electricity out—and one of Charlie's giant chickens a charred and melted mess: A vendor had left an electric fan running. The appliance had short-circuited and turned the colossal cluck into a flaming kabob.

Montana Charlie's Little America never lost popularity. Wells Petroleum and Refiners Pride were sold after Charlie's death—and Charlie's Welco Truck Stop on Route 66 went bust—but the flea market survives to this day. On summer Sundays, 450 to 500 dealers hawk their wares at Little America. Chicago refugees whittle away weekends moseying around the displays. The man who loved Montana would be pleased with the rural escape his flea market affords. Charlie himself always kept a few horses in the Land of Lincoln. Into his autumn years, he rode every Sunday.

"He was very creative. And, God damn, his word was good," Chuck Reid says of his father. "He really liked working. I never heard him say he was tired. A couple times I heard him say he was bushed, but I never heard him use the word tired."

Montana Charlie Reid rode into life's sunset on July 31, 1982. If justice rules our world, he was met at the Pearly Gates by a horse, a chorus of clowns and a calliope. Whether Charlie gave the steam pipes a toot remains anyone's guess. Smart money says he did something to stir up the soupy harp music.

Even if he only hummed *Home on the Range.*

Above: A worker walks Montana Charlie's Little America before the Sunday morning crush.

Below: Montana Charlie at his Burnt Leather Ranch.

Rossi friends and family members dance a dance of hospitality for Rossi's Ballroom at Eagle Park.

Rossi's Ballroom at Eagle Park

At the corner of Front Street and Route 66, the sounds of industry go galloping on.

The blind horse that powered the first factory is gone, replaced in turn by rhythmic engines of steam and gasoline. Slow-moving screw presses have succumbed to the hymn of hydraulics. Mixers knock out noodles as sleek as saxophones.

A rough mile and a half down the highway, Peter Rossi steps through the doors of his ballroom and into the Illinois air. The guttural crunch and punch of midget boxers follows him—buoyed on the breeze by this country's absolute quiet. Time was, Rossi could spend a peaceful hour before an evening's first set feeding his eagle. Time was, the rhythm of the night came only from tangos and turkey trots.

Overhead, the moon cuts through the clouds—rolling across time and the tree tops—an egg-colored cog above an industrial world. For a moment, the sounds of progress melt romantic inside Rossi's mind. Perhaps, tomorrow, he will book Benny Goodman. Perhaps, tomorrow, he will build something that will change the flow of traffic on this old road. For now, the sky bows grandly in melancholy blue. At ten o'clock the dancers take the floor.

And this night looks lovely for a waltz.

legance and architecture will always dance together on Route 66. Striking up turrets or steeples or spires, the architect lifts the shoulders of the old road, and the road whirls with grace as it leaps from town to town.

In Braidwood, Illinois, the Rossi family raised roofs almost from the moment their feet found this country. Their patriarch, Peter Rossi, Sr., was born in 1851 in Busano, Italy. He spent his early life as a government employee specializing in grain milling and macaroni manufacturing. In 1876, he opened his own noodle factory in his native town.

In 1878, Peter Rossi, Sr. immigrated to Braidwood, Illinois. He worked as a check weighman for the Crumby Mine before opening Braidwood's first hardware business. In 1886, he founded the Peter Rossi Macaroni Factory on Braidwood's 4th Street near Division. The plant later moved into the old Broadbent Hotel on 1st Street— and the buzzing shoulders of Route 66.

Peter's son, Stephen, came of age on the Mother Road's shoulders. As a youth, Stephen sold pocket knives door-to-door. As an adult, he opened the Stephen Rossi Saloon on the south side of Braidwood's Main Street west of the railroad tracks. "Spaghetti" Rossi—as pals and pasta lovers called Stephen—maintained a free lunch in the back of his saloon for regular customers. He sold beer at a nickel a bucket. In 1920, after Prohibition blew the foam off his steins, Stephen opened a grocery. A gasoline pump sprouted in front of the store, and the family so skilled at stuffing stomachs began filling fuel tanks as well.

Fortune left Stephen's son, Peter, to discover the road's curious side. One fine Braidwood day, an eagle fell out of the sky. The regal bird was crippled and would never fly again. Young Peter became the bird's adopted pop. Soon an iron cage stood in the empty lot adjacent to Stephen's grocery, and the young Peter Rossi embarked on a career of roadside entertainment.

MGM CORPORATION OF AMERICA
NEW YORK · CHICAGO · LOS ANGELES
PRESENTS

Maurie
Sherman
AND HIS
ORCHESTRA

ROSSI'S PARK
BRAIDWOOD, ILL., ON ROUTE 4
SUN. MAY 7TH
—— Admission ——
Gent's 40c; Ladies' 35; Dancing Free

COMING:
Clyde McCoy .... **May 14th**
Ralph Bennett .... **May 21**
OPEN AIR MOVIES SOON. :: W.L.S. BARN DANCE, MAY 11th.

"The one wing drooped," says old-time Braidwood eagle-watcher Bernice Schoppe. "But when they captured that eagle and put it in this great big cage, it was a novelty. At first, they kept the eagle in Braidwood. I would pass it on my way to school, and I remember I was half afraid of it. This eagle was a strong bird; it would come at you if you got too close to the cage. Later, Petey moved the eagle out to the grounds where he would build his dance hall. That's why he called the place Eagle Park."

Peter Rossi christened Eagle Park in the middle 1920s, hanging his hopes—and his best bird—on a clearing of trees southwest of town. Peter's younger brother, John, became Peter's partner. In 1927, Rossi's Ballroom at Eagle Park opened its floor.

The Rossi's built their ballroom in the grip of Prohibition and during what could be called the Day of the Dance Hall. Taverns stood empty; beer gardens ran dry, and folks frequented dance halls simply to slip some music into their lives. Although Peter etched a baseball diamond onto the back of the property, elegance ruled Eagle Park. An intricate leaf-pattern speckled the dance hall's facade. Stone planters poked posies at noses, and a small rock wall added artful intrigue. Peter placed his eagle a short distance from the hall. Slow-dancing couples found in the bird the perfect excuse to skip a beat and step outside. The grounds of Eagle Park were well-treed and took on a wispy, otherworldly quality after dark.

"It was quite the place, this Eagle Park," says Bernice Schoppe. "I remember there was a lot of white and a lot of light brown in the dance hall's design. The inside was beautiful. As you came in, you saw a small office that Petey kept. The stage was huge, and they had seats surrounding the dance floor. If you didn't dance, you could sit in the bleachers and enjoy the music. So many people came just to hear the bands—just to sit in the bleachers."

From its beginning, Rossi's Ballroom booked the finest bands Chicago could offer. Peter and John or father Stephen routinely motored to the Windy City and engaged acts from the Music Corporation of America. Groups on their way to the bright lights of big cities slipped in for a gig and traveling money—among them Danny Russo, Art Kassel's Radio Band and the Jimmy Raschel Orchestra. On other evenings, fainter stars shone, and bands from nearby Joliet filled the boogie bill. Farmer's Dances offered free cider and doughnuts to those who attended in barn-yard clothes. Maggie Rossi opened a lunch-room on premises. *The Gardner Chronicle* invited all to "Dance—Donce—Dine" at Rossi's Ballroom.

Over the dance floor, a large sphere sparkled with colored lights. The elegant ball had been plucked from a building at the Chicago World's Fair. On one occasion, it blinked sleepy tints over the most exhaustive exhibition of dancing Will County had ever seen: Marathon dancers took to Rossi's Ballroom in 1931 to sashay and snore their way through ten days of footwork. The contest lasted a blistering 252 1/2 hours. Afterward, the final five couples were shuffled in front of cameras for posterity's curios eye.

At Rossi's Ballroom, Peter Rossi him-self took every opportunity to encourage revelers to their feet. The squat little man with the spring in his samba loved to teach by example, and he took to the dance floor at every available drop of a downbeat.

"My father was a short, little man, but he could sure twirl the floor," says Peter's daughter, Mary Ogg. "He loved orchestra music. I mean, he *loved* it. When he danced, he preferred to fox-trot."

Opposite and right: Rossi's Ballroom posters—artful exercises in their own right.

EARL GRAY
- AND HIS -
ORCHESTRA

Featuring
The Three
Balladiers
Plus a Brilliant
Vocal Ensemble

Music from the Modern Viewpoint

ROSSI'S BALL ROOM
BRAIDWOOD, ROUTE 66
Sunday Evening, June 23

ALSO ANOTHER
AMATEUR NIGHT

Admission: Ladies 10c; Gents 25c.   No other charge.

DANCING EVERY SUNDAY NIGHT
CENTRAL SHOW PTG. CO. MASON CITY, IOWA

Rossi's Ballroom enjoyed lucrative returns into the later 1920s and early 1930s. Peter and John built a service station on the property and added cabins for overnight guests. Peter's eagle died, and the grounds were renamed Rossi's Park. Prohibition ended, and ballroom attendance dwindled. Newborn taverns offered heated competition. The Rossis turned to gimmicks to keep their gala going.

"Roy Gordon played at Rossi's," recalls Bernice Schoppe. "Roy was a bandleader from Joliet. One night, Petey came over to me, and he asked me, 'Will you dance with Roy Gordon? He wants to take a little break.' Roy and I got out on the floor, and they brought out all these lights and this movie camera. They started filming us. That became a big thing: movies for the crowd's enjoyment."

The Rossis made their grandest stand against the rebirth of bars when they began screening Open Air Vitaphone movies. The sometimes-silent, sometimes-talking flicks were hawked as a perfect way to beat summer heat. Unwilling to lose customers to a dance hall, the Morris Theatre began billing itself as "70 degrees cool." The Blackstone Theatre in Dwight settled the score by booking an appearance by Simplicio and Lucio the Siamese Twins—with their beautiful dancing brides.

On Thanksgiving evening of 1933, Rossi's Ballroom took what in retrospect may be seen as its last formidable swing at survival. That night, the park became the site of one of the biggest boxing shows ever to bruise Braidwood. Ladies were invited. A dance after the show began at 10 p.m.

The service station on the grounds of Rossi Park pumped an average of 5,000 to 6,000 gallons of gas a month in the later 1920s.

The program itself featured seven bouts of boxing, including a finale that pitted Russell Kamp ("Kankakee's 135 lb. Wonder") against Otto Geisholt ("Dwight's 135 lb. Fighting Dutchman"). A warm-up bout by midget boxers started the carnage. Tiny lumps rained on all.

By the time fire flared at Rossi's Ballroom in 1935, Peter Rossi had lowered his dance hall admission price to ten cents. The conflagration—started when a painter left a can of color too close to a stove—destroyed little that wasn't already dead.

Without Rossi's Ballroom, Braidwood tiptoed forward. So did Peter Rossi. The man who had built a dance hall in a nondescript grove had many more structures to build. In 1939, Braidwood's alignment of Route 66 was rerouted. Peter personally laid the foundation of a new Rossi Service Station that would take 75% of its business from tourists and pump 30,000 gallons of petrol per month. Next to the station, the Rossis constructed a restaurant that they leased to the Weitz brothers of Morris, Illinois.

In 1950, the Rossi's built the Rossi Motel—once regarded as the largest and best sleeping spot in southwestern Will County. Peter Rossi raised his last establishment in Joliet—a restaurant/motel/banquet room with an indoor swimming pool. Peter called this last project Autumn Acres. Today, the complex serves the Joliet Elks Club.

Time has proved the perfect test for Rossi architecture. Of the buildings in which Peter took a planner's hand, all but the Eagle Park structures survive.

Above: In February of 1950, the Rossis were honored as Sinclair Oil's Merchants of the Month. From left: Peter, John, Maggie and Stephen Rossi.

Below: Rossi's Motel, 1950.

The old strip of road at Route 66 and Highway 113 could accurately be called Rossi's Row, filled as it is with Rossi's Service Station, the Weitz Cafe and Rossi's Motel. The buildings stand disguised as Lucenta Tire, the Braidwood Laundromat and the Braidwood Motel, but underneath their modern facades they remain monuments to a man who was at his best in the middle of a fox trot—and trophies to an architect who would advise anyone to take progress by the hand and lead it to music into graceful and high-kicking dreams.

Violet Grush, daughter of Riviera founder Jim Girot, tangled with bootleggers, Tom Mix and one obnoxious, operatic parrot during her Riviera days.

The Riviera

Al Capone Passed Gas Here in 1932
　　　—Riviera Men's Room sign

it stops will always play a prominent part in highway driving. Craving eggs over-easy, forty winks or stretching time, the urge to stop and sniff the snapdragons hits hard and hits often, taxing brake pedals, tight schedules and the patience of parents who told kids to go before they climbed into the car. What revs up, must wind down remains the road's only infallible rule, and the piggiest road hog is the soonest puttering curbside to poop out. Nowhere east of Gardner, Illinois, can the pause that refreshes be taken in more fanciful fashion than inside the restrooms of the roadhouse Riviera.

"Local kids write about our toilets in their school newspapers," Riviera owner Peggy Kraft says. "They say the toilets were built as high as they are so Al Capone wouldn't get shot in the back."

Dodging water levels—or plunger-packing hit men—the potties at the Riviera stand cocked to crapper heaven. Reached via a series of concrete steps that seem set on scaling Mount Everest, the lofty loos could cause nosebleeds in those unaccustomed to squatting atop crater rims. The commode in the Men's Room—where the tribute tells of Al Capone blasting his best—can intimidate any rump, but it's the bowl inside the Ladies' Room that truly bullies buttocks. Affectionately known as The Throne, the rocketing pedestal seems destined to tempt a tinkle from Mir astronauts.

The towering toilets are only two indications the Riviera achieved sentience decades ago—and promptly lost its mind. Walls commonly have ears, but the puffs of crisp, cavernous air that waft

The Riviera's infamous Throne: a place to pause and ponder on gangsters who have come and gone.

through the Riveria suggest its partitions hide a bucketful of lungs and other twitching organs.

Patched together like a Frankenstein monster that lost its own assembly instructions, the Riviera survives as the wonderfully skewered vision of Jim Girot—a South Wilmington saloon keeper who built by his hunches and found his strongest urge along Route 4 where the highway met the Mazon River.

"As the Depression was beginning, all the stores in our hometown of South Wilmington were closing," recalls Girot's daughter, Violet Grush. "The land on which the Riviera stands today was all trees. My family passed it on trips to Joliet. My father would always stop and say, 'I'm going to build me a place on this spot.' And my mother would tell him, 'You're not going to move me into the woods!'"

But into the woods the Girot family went, dragging along a payroll office from a defunct South Wilmington coal mine and an empty Gardner church that had seen more graceful days. Girot hired hands to help him dig, called the hole a cellar and tacked together church and coal office over it.

The year was 1928 when the Riviera reared its humpback into the Illinois sky.

From its opening, the building led a lucky life. Girot had swapped stock for the property, stock that amounted to less than a booby prize after the topple of '29.

While Prohibition raged, the Riviera remained wet—working with a peephole admittance policy and law enforcement officials who never let a badge interfere with their beer bellies. The close proximity of a rumrunner named Jimmy the Bear fueled rumors that Al Capone made the Riviera his regular watering hole—or at least loped in for an occasional leak.

The Riviera in its salad days. The woman standing on the steps is longtime employee, Clara Bruns.

Copyright 1934   Printed in   U.S.A.

Price
$1.00

foods
and
fashions
of 1935

Compliments of
THE RIVIERA
on Route 4
Gardner, Ill.

"A BUMPER CROP"

YOU ARE
Always WELCOME at

RIVIERA
SPECIAL DINNERS
FROG LEGS
CHICKEN & STEAKS
JIM GIROT, Prop.
ALT. U. S. 66
GARDNER, ILL.
PHONE 3021

CLOSE COVER BEFORE STRIKING

Riviera advertising often implied the most succulent legs at the roadhouse weren't necessarily on the frogs.

"Jimmy the Bear's relatives were from Cicero," recalls Violet. "I think that's where people got the connection to Al Capone. But who knows? Maybe Al Capone *was* down here. Anybody I ask says, 'Oh, yeah, he was here. I drove the getaway car.'"

Inside its odd walls, the Riviera flip-flopped and folded back on itself so many times diners needed compasses to locate their seats. The old coal office safe became a walk-in cooler, and Girot's chance meeting with a traveling scenic painter resulted in a stubble of papier-mache stalactites that still pimples the ceiling over the bar. The building's upstairs—that today serves as the Riviera's kitchen—originally served as the restaurant's eating area, and those who found it were treated to the best counter service in Grundy County, courtesy of Mrs. Girot. Tom Mix munched toast there one evening after poking the nose of his Rolls Royce into the parking lot. ("He came in with a gal friend, and he told me to get a good education," Violet remembers.) On another starstruck occasion, Gene Kelly twinkled by on his way to Tinseltown.

"That was when there were gas pumps out front," relates Peggy Kraft. "Gene Kelly stopped to fill his car with gas. He had a yellow or white convertible with wire wheels. And he told the attendant, 'I'm on my way to Hollywood, and I'm going to be famous! You'll see my name in lights some day!' He gave the attendant a dollar tip and went dancing across the parking lot. The attendant thought, 'That guy's nuts.'"

Other acts sideswiped the Riviera's stage. Violet's brother Larry opened a small zoo on premises after adopting a batch of baby fox. "We had raccoons that would frisk your pockets for peanuts," Violet remembers, "and we had a polly parrot. Some old woman in South Wilmington had this polly parrot, and she'd sing opera to it all the time. When she passed away, her son gave the parrot to my mother. So we had that thing in here singing its head off."

With Prohibition past, the Riviera hit full stride. Orchestras boomed, folks waded three-deep at the bar and frog legs became the delicacy of the day. Dinners were now served downstairs, and hoppers took their last ride from kitchen to table on a dumbwaiter that Girot had installed between floors. Amphibians awaiting their turn on a plate did time full-bodied and frozen in one of four holes of a five-hole ice cream freezer. The last hole was reserved for traditional vanilla.

Territorial disputes erupted over slot machines. Girot originally installed his own one-armed bandits inside the Riviera—and found them quickly replaced by slot machines owned by local political bigwigs. The bigwigs' machines were in turn supplanted by machines owned by enterprising thugs, and so on—until no one could tell whose cherries were whose. At worst, the Riviera was raided during off hours, and machines were battered to bits. On slightly better days, midnight cowboys rode into town—and stopped all business while they broke out their tools.

"Me and my cousin were cooking frog legs one night," says Violet, "and all of a sudden there was this guy standing by the door. 'Stay where you're at,' he says to us. And we knew we'd better. The old frog legs were jumping in the pan, but we just stood there while they took the machines out downstairs."

In fairness, Violet points out, not all of the racketeers had hearts of steel. Puffy Burt—one of the first and fairest—gave away thermometers as Christmas gifts to show his good will toward men. Puffy's last surviving bit of mercury hangs today behind the Riviera's bar—directly above the dumbwaiter's doors.

In 1950, Jim Girot died of smoke inhalation after battling a blaze that began as a Riviera grease fire. The fire fried stalactites and temporarily closed the roadhouse, but Girot had saved his crossbred baby. His wife, Rose, remarried, and the Riviera waddled on. Violet returned routinely to cook. In 1972, Rose sold the Riviera to longtime Chicago saloonkeepers Bob and Peggy Kraft. The Krafts tacked a shower curtain to the back room ceiling, carpeted one wall and installed several strings of light-up monkeys. Violet still returned to cook.

Today the Riviera survives as a fossilized funhouse—and a slap in the pan to anyone who thinks Route 66 never amounted to more than wrathful grapes. Far from fading into the moonlight, the Riviera's quirks have sharpened with age. Regulars still hunch at the bar as if instinctively protecting themselves from parts of the building that might pop off. Waitresses dart in and out of the coal office safe that will chill jello till Kingdom Come. And the toilets still seem as if they're perched light years above their floors.

"The Riviera has an individual past," Violet reasons of the Riviera's success. "It's a friendly place, and it's always been different. I would say that says a lot. I tell friends, you've got to do your own thing as you go along in life. Otherwise you end up old and crabby."

Inside the Men's Room—and perched commodiously on one of the Riviera's two thrones—the ghost of Al Capone sits. The toilet tissue waves within reach, but the echo of smashing slot machines—and something in the smell of frog legs—tells this spook it's better to remain still. It shudders at the rumble of the dumbwaiter—worries for all the talk it hears of stalactites and light-up monkeys. Then realizes—looking earthward from its mile-high seat—that for years it's been quite afraid to come down.

Right: Green glow the monkeys in the Riviera's Terrace Room.

Below: Behind the bar and under the stalactites, current Riviera owners Bob and Peggy Kraft welcome all.

Fly Fly Fly

Aeroplane Flights

At the Air Port 1 Mile North of the Log Cabin on
Route No. 4, Pontiac, Ill.

SAT.-SUN., June 22-23

Regular Rates $2.50 Per Person

Extra Special
For Saturday and Sunday
Pay For Your Weight

The rate for carrying passengers these two days
will be 1 cent per pound for your weight. No passenger carried less than $1.00.

THIS IS YOUR CHANCE—
DON'T MISS IT!

Left: A 1929 Joe Seloti ad offers to take
passengers up, up and away.

Below: The magnificent man with his
flying machine.

The Talking Crow at the Log Cabin Inn & the Pontiac Air Circus

Upon the pages of folklore, few birds take the beating of the common crow. Aesop calls the Crow an avian idiot. Shakespeare consigns him to a rooky wood, and Noah boots him off the ark before the holy boat hits dry land. While cartoonists Heckle and Jeckle him, Mother Goose bakes him breathing into four-and-twenty pies. So little do we respect this simple, cawing soul, that at those times we engage him in all-out agricultural war, we send soldiers of straw.

But once upon a time—in Pontiac, Illinois—one crow commanded a bit of birdie respect. One crow ordered hors d'oeuvres—and told the cook to put some meat on his buns.

"They used to say the crow's tongue was split," Marjorie O'Brien says of the Talking Crow of Pontiac. "That crow talked a blue streak. And you could talk *with* him."

The tale of the Talking Crow of Pontiac begins in the fields of the Old World. The Selotis were Italian immigrants who came to these United States to mine coal in Illinois. While above ground, Victor and Rosa Seloti reared a flock of five boys and three girls. Two of their brood—Joe and younger brother Victor, Jr., or "Babe"—turned to the roadside to make their living. In 1926, they opened a service station on a patch of Route 4 that became Route 66. Next to the station, they built a cafe—of trees.

"The public service would discard telephone poles after they used 'em," says Pontiac old-timer, Hubert Boswell. "The Seloti boys knew who had these poles. So they bought a bunch, notched 'em and put 'em together. From the beginning, their plan was to make the buildings look like old log cabins. That's why they called the cafe the Log Cabin Inn."

While Babe tended dipsticks and blown tires, Joe slung hash at the woody cafe. Barbecue became a house specialty. Joe personally manned the barbecue pit, an enormous Hades of charcoal and sparks enclosed in a small shed. Smokehouse windows afforded all a view of the spitted hams turning inside. On the back of this smokehouse, Joe fashioned a pen for his talking pet crow.

Throughout his life, Joe Seloti found fascination with things that flew—or came feather-close to taking off. As a teenager, he trooped with Ed A. Evans Shows—a motorcycle stunt man for the formidable carnival group. Joe spent World War I scootering through Coblenz, Germany. Back home, he bought one of the original French taxicabs that in 1914 had transported troops to the first battle of Marne. Joe ever after drove that taxi to American Legion conventions throughout the states.

The Talking Crow of Pontiac enjoys a birdie brew.

Land of Lincoln logs: The Log Cabin Station and the Log Cabin Inn.

In an age of aviation, Joe cast an eager eye on the wild blue yonder. He bought a Waco 10 biplane, christened it *Miss Pontiac* and parked it on an area farm while he built Pontiac's first airport. The hub sat on 87 acres along Route 66 one mile north of the Log Cabin Inn. Joe built the airport's hanger at a cost of $2,000. He covered its 4,200-foot runway with shale and oiled and compacted cinders.

Joe Seloti realized his airy love could make him money. In 1931, when the Forrest Bank was robbed, the sheriff of Livingston County paid Joe $20 to fly down the thief. On Sundays, Joe offered airplane rides to anyone at a cost of $1 each—$2 for sight-seeing trips around Pontiac. Airport classes were offered in navigation and meteorology. Pilots Fred Bartlett and Thomas Woods taught students to fly. Periodically, Joe orchestrated a Pontiac Air Circus.

"Next to the Log Cabin, there was a tourist park," recalls Joe's daughter, Dorothy Zaubi. "During the air circus, twin brothers named Seabourne camped there. The Seabournes came from San Antonio. They performed parachute jumps. My father paid them so much per jump. They would race each other to the ground."

Robert and Herbert—the 19-year-old Seabourne twins—were joined in their antics by pilots from across Illinois. The Pontiac Air Circus became a recurring event filled with balloon burstings, bomb droppings and a 25-mile race. Brooks and Bell, the "daredevils of the air," defied death at 5,000 feet.

Art Carnahan, a pilot from Bloomington, flew upside-down and navigated a glider over crowds.

Joe Seloti and friends flew the frenzied skies over other Illinois towns. In spite of their early-day equipment, aerial mishaps were few. On one occasion, Art Carnahan dove to save jumper Florence Palmer Davis after her chute caught on the tail of his plane and tore in two. Carnahan hoped to wrap the cords of her chute in his wing struts, but Mrs. Davis landed in an oat field and sank more than a foot into the ground.

The Pontiac Air Circus flipped and twirled its way into the 1930s until the day the Pontiac Airport burned. The fire destroyed Joe Seloti's *Miss Pontiac* and a Curtiss J1 Robin owned by Joe's brother Babe. Joe commiserated with his talking pet crow.

Joe Seloti and his Parisian taxi shuttle Will Rogers around an American Legion convention in Los Angeles.

Joe Seloti's Pontiac Airport was, in its day, larger than the airport at Bloomington, Illinois.

No one remembers who discovered the Talking Crow of Pontiac. Dorothy Zaubi recalls only that her father received the crow from an elderly judge and took pains to teach the bird the art of articulation. The gift of gab is a tricky thing to give a crow. Seloti's success still amazes, particularly if one believes the Talking Crow of Pontiac mastered a modest sense of syntax. This bird was more than a mimic, supporters insist. This bird possessed a working vocabulary.

"That bird could carry a conversation," insists Marjorie O'Brien. "I'm not kidding one bit. He was most verbal when Joe was cooking. That's when he'd holler that he wanted something to eat. He always knew exactly what he wanted. He really was something to see."

A rare photograph shows an air circus in which Joe Seloti played part.

The Talking Crow spun his best soliloquies during summer months. In fair weather, beer drinkers imbibed at picnic tables in back of the Log Cabin Inn, lugging outside the only alcohol sold on site. The Talking Crow developed a taste for malted beverages, and he learned to mix small talk with his drinking. Uninitiated boozers were occasionally frightened when they found Seloti's featherbrain staring at them and apparently calling out names.

In time, the Talking Crow of Pontiac became a popular roadside personality. Customers stopping for gas or a nibble would hear him squawking his avian English and linger to investigate. Those making the acquaintance of the wordy bird often visited him on subsequent trips. Today, no method exists by which to measure the amount of business the Talking Crow of Pontiac brought to the Log Cabin Inn. For his part, the crow continued to pipe up until old age stilled his babbling beak—and sent him to that Great Canary Cage in the Sky.

Edgar Allan Poe played patsy to a rapping raven. Camelot owned Archimedes, an orating owl. But only Route 66 through north-central Illinois retained the Talking Crow of Pontiac. In back of the old Log Cabin Inn, where the scent of barbecue once bullied all beaks, the fast-talking crow may be gone. So may be the air circus that once rolled up the street. But the spirit of both lingers on in the feeling one finds soaring past fence posts in this state. Bank your wings onto Illinois Route 66. And fly away fantastic.

Coney Island's Dreamland Park: The first amusement park in the world built with an eye on art and large, naked angels.

Dreamland Park

In 1904, former Republican New York State Senator William H. Reynolds opened Dreamland Park along Coney Island's ticklish midsection. The senator painted Dreamland's towers a pristine snow white, and opened the world's first amusement park dedicated to art, architecture and elegance.

Roughly two decades later, Basel Edgar Chattin—a businessman from southern Indiana—raised Dreamland Park on Route 4 leaving Pontiac, Illinois. Chattin painted his ballroom and concession stand a pristine snow white and invited all dancers to appreciate the park's art and architecture.

There the similarity ends.

"My father had two left feet," confides Chattin's daughter, Paula O'Bryan. "There's nothing elegant about that."

The Dreamland Park of Pontiac, Illinois—the Dreamland of Route 4 and later Route 66—was built as a large, alluring ballroom in crop country—an informal stomping ground for farmers and field hands, but one instilled with an otherworldly grace. Against the silos of Livingston County, Dreamland's ivory facade stood out like an albino udder. But it also stood as intriguing as an iceberg in a barn.

Dreamland Park found its beat in the heart of the Jazz Age and during a time when the Charleston and the Tiger Rag wrung buckets of sweat from dancers. One of the biggest draws of Chattin's ballroom could be found in its hinged walls that raised or lowered at the drop of a thermometer. Once opened, the portals encouraged prancers to take a spin on the outside pavilion. Patrons could park their rumps on benches dotting the banks of Rooks Creek or stroll to a snack stand for soft drinks. "My father was dead set against liquor," Paula O'Bryan says.

"At Dreamland's concession stand, no one got anything harder than root beer."

Dreamland's steamy insides were a study in scant decor. Clunky benches lined walls. A small bandstand boogied at building's front. As years rolled by—and Chattin occasionally booked vaudeville acts—the benches were rearranged to provide a common viewpoint from which folks could watch funnies. On dance nights the corners of the floor were policed by strict ticket takers.

"Monday morning, Mom and I would help Dad count the nickels and dimes we made on each dance," says Paula O'Bryan. "We'd sit and roll the coins. I remember that very well.

"I loved to go to Dreamland," Paula continues. "The men who worked for dad would dance with me, and I thought that was big stuff. There was an older caretaker who had a house on the property. He and his family lived there, and I often danced with him. But my mother was careful about how often I went to Dreamland. I never went on a school night."

As the roaring twenties gave way to the whimpering thirties, Basel Edgar Chattin's Dreamland Park burned to the ground. In 1911, Dreamland Park on Coney Island had met a similar end. The cause of the fire that destroyed Chattin's Dreamland was never determined. The blaze that burned Coney's Dreamland sparked in an amusement ride called Hell Gate and left lions with manes aflame roaring through streets. Today, in one final, feline echo, stray tabbies scurry across the driveways that once led to Chattin's Dreamland. They run from revelers who will never arrive, scatting from a fire that fizzled with the Jazz Age, but somehow suggest—with tails arrogantly raised—there's still a hot time to be had in the old town tonight.

The Lincoln Assassination—one of nine moments captured in wax—at the A. Lincoln Wax Museum.

A. Lincoln Wax Museum

our score and about a dozen decades ago, Abraham Lincoln drew first breath in a cabin near Hodgenville, Kentucky. Springfield, Illinois, has gone ga-ga for him ever since. In the Illinois state capitol, Lincoln attractions breed like Kennedys and grow bigger than Tafts—biting out whole blocks in the bustling downtown area. Between Tomb and Home, you can sneak like Nixon into the Lincoln-Herndon Law Offices,

run like Willkie past the Lincoln Depot or count *I Like Ike* buttons at 6th Street and Washington with the aid of the Lincoln Ledger. And before you're Honest-Abed to death, you can Gerald Ford flop into First Presbyterian and land on the Lincoln Pew.

On the southeast corner of 9th Street and Capitol Avenue, the A. Lincoln Wax Museum once reared its bearded heads. The anatomically-correct dreamchild of Hank Geving—it found a partner in Springfield newspaper mogul J.R. "Bud" Fitzpatrick—and lived

Hank Geving, sculptor and wunderkind behind the A. Lincoln Wax Museum.

on land over which Lincoln never walked, never talked and—presumably—never much noticed. Yet from 1971 to the late 1980s, the A. Lincoln Wax Museum carried more than a passing candle for the Great Emancipator. Before the final tip of its top hat, it gained fame as the only wax museum in the world dedicated to one man—and proved positively that character in the flesh is the hardest thing to carve.

Hank Geving was a native of New Richmond, Wisconsin, a self-professed romantic with an eye for the visual arts. Out of high school, he moved to Madison and pursued a career as a television cameraman. An experiment sketching famous personalities for broadcast news betrayed a natural drawing talent and attracted the eyes of others.

"My news director asked me if I'd done any sculpting," Geving recounts. "The summer home of Ringling Bros. Circus is in Wisconsin Dells, and he had long thought of starting a Circus Wax Museum. I had never sculpted, but I was willing to try. I went over to his home one Saturday, and we went into Madison and bought a couple hundred pounds of clay. The first wax figures I completed were figures planned for this museum: Phineas Taylor Barnum and Buffalo Bill Cody and Tom Thumb."

Circus life can be frightening. When the day came for financial commitment, Geving's partner declined to make the monetary investment necessary to start a Circus Wax Museum. Geving left for Los Angeles to pursue his career as a camera operator in the larger television market. He stumbled into a job at the Stuberg-Keller Studio in Burbank—at the time one of the leading wax mannequin manufacturers in the world. Geving was amazed to learn the wax sculpting process he'd developed over the past year was similar to theirs—with one important difference. "I used a microcrystalline wax," Geving explains, "and they still used beeswax. My microcrystalline blend had a higher melting temperature, and that eliminated the sag problem you normally experience with wax figures."

A season's colors came and went. In 1970, Geving returned to the Midwest, taking a job under his original news director in Waterloo, Iowa. By this time, he'd set his sights on raising his own wax museum and turned to history in search of subjects.

"I've always been enamored with Abraham Lincoln," Geving says of his choice of the 16th president. "I began planning a Life of Lincoln Museum that would follow Lincoln from boyhood to death."

Common sense governed Geving's choice of locations for his museum-to-be. He studied tourist flows, discovered the Lincoln Heritage Trail was the number three tourist destination in the country, and aimed squarely for Springfield, Illinois.

Geving cleared a space in his duplex basement and began creating an army of Abes. He fashioned chests, pelvises and limbs of papier-mache, and he hired a University of Wisconsin costume designer to dress the trunks. Antique stores were raided for props. Geving's first wife, Andrea, implanted human hair into each skull one to three strands at a time.

Geving began to look for a building and a backer for his A. Lincoln Wax Museum. He found both on a weekend trip to Springfield, Illinois. J.R. "Bud" Fitzpatrick was a Springfield Somebody, a wheeler-dealer who published a newspaper called *The Mainstreet* and dipped his interest into real estate. By coincidence, one of *his* desires had for years been the development of a museum dedicated to the life of Abraham Lincoln. When Fitzpatrick met Geving, a partnership was born.

"Fitzpatrick was very excited," Geving remembers. "He had the real estate across the street from Lincoln's Home. He put up the money, and I spent the next few months finishing the figures. My father was a carpenter. I sent him to Springfield for two months and into this old ex-post office that Fitzpatrick owned. We worked out the museum's layout over the phone."

In preparation of their presidential opening, Geving and Andrea loaded up their truck and moved to Lincoln Land. The journey to Springfield occurred under cover of darkness to protect their pack of presidents from the bipartisan sun. Several nights later, all Abes were ready for visitors. Geving slept fitfully on the museum's floor. "The building had no in-built alarm system," Geving recalls, "but a local company graciously lent us a few motion sensors. We rigged these to sound through a radio in the event of trouble, and two or three times during the night that radio came on.

The A. Lincoln Wax Museum as it appeared in September of 1971.

"I was sleeping next to Ulysses S. Grant and Robert E. Lee—the Appomattox diorama. I literally took the sword out of General Lee's scabbard and spent the rest of the night with the saber next to me. *Something* out there was moving."

The A. Lincoln Wax Museum opened August 7, 1971, and quickly earned fame for its accurate depictions. Civil War scholars loped through the Lincolns and pronounced Geving's work precise. The Springfield paper sang praises for figures historically pure, down to popped vest buttons. And an excited patron told Geving what the latter had never known: that the museum's concept was itself unique. Never before had a wax museum traced the life of one man. The 18 mannequins and nine tableaus that progressed chronologically—from Abe-as-a-boy, to Lincoln as clerk, to the Lincoln-Douglas debates, Inauguration, Emancipation Proclamation, Gettysburg address, surrender of Lee and Lincoln assassination—were artistic firsts.

Along the aisles carpeted kingly red, there existed personal touches only the sculptor could appreciate. "In the first diorama, I modeled Thomas Lincoln, Lincoln's father, after my father, Wesley,"

Geving says. "Then I used my first wife, Andrea, as Ann Rutledge in the store scene. The other head I really liked was Zachary Taylor. I sculpted Zachary Taylor—then used him as the telegrapher in the telegraph office."

Over the years, the bevy of cool bodies suffered unique problems. On one occasion, Abe's head fell off in the Gettysburg Address scene. The blown top caused quite a stir until a little old lady stepped forward. "I hate to complain, but Mr. Lincoln's head is on the floor in there," she told the management, and shuffled back to her sightseeing.

"We had problems with hands," admits later-day museum owner Mary "Betsy" Burton. "People would steal hands. Kids would break off fingers and toes. And hats—my goodness—I had to replace four or five top hats a year."

As time passed, macabre souvenir hunters became the least of the museum's worries. On February 1, 1972, the Gevings filed a $50,000 lawsuit against Fitzpatrick, charging that he had not paid their salaries or for the building's remodeling and had not incorporated the business as provided for in their signed agreement. They further charged

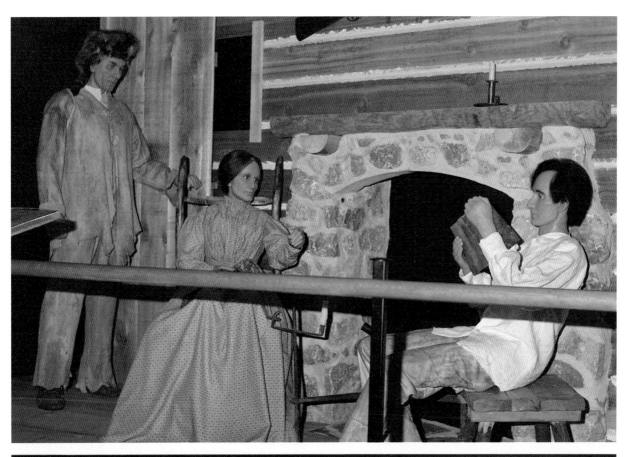

Fitzpatrick with holding their sculpting tools and their mannequins. Fitzpatrick had locked the Gevings out of the museum. His daughter and son-in-law, Mary "Betsy" and Thomas Burton, were minding the melt-ables.

"At the end of the trial, the jury came in and asked the judge if they had to stick with the amount of money that we had asked for in the lawsuit," Geving remembers. "The judge said, 'No,' and the jury said, 'Then we're going to award the Gevings much more because this man really took them.'"

The jury awarded the Gevings $93,800. Under the settlement, the A. Lincoln Wax Museum—and its inventory of Abes—remained with the Burtons. For their part, the Burtons maintained the A. Lincoln Wax Museum with considerable care and pride—adding four dioramas and completing an expansion project that nearly doubled the museum's size in the spring of 1977. But a visit to the A. Lincoln Wax Museum would never again be the unique artistic experience it had been with its self-taught sculptor in residence.

Geving moved back to California. He continued to practice his craft. He sculpted a Franklin Delano Roosevelt head that appeared in the television mini-series *Franklin and Eleanor,* and he designed several dioramas in honor of the country's bicentennial. Geving completed his last commissioned sculpting job in the later 1970s—creating a number of noggins for a Sports Hall of Fame. "When I finished the last three heads, I decided I would personally take them over to their studio," Geving says. "And here was this kid with a gouging tool carving character lines into the faces I'd made. He told me, 'We've decided we don't want to spend a lot of money on lighting, so we need to increase these character lines.' Since I was such a romantic, I decided at that point I would never sculpt on commission again."

In 1987, the Lincoln Home in Springfield was closed for restoration. The shutdown devastated the A. Lincoln Wax Museum which had for years passed out discount coupons to Lincoln Home visitors. Not long afterward, the Burtons closed the museum, sold the building and moved the mannequins into storage. The entire collection sans assassination scene sold to the Lincoln Museum in Hodgenville, Kentucky. The Assassination Scene sold to the Museum of the Southwest between Dallas and Fort Worth, Texas. It subsequently perished in a fire.

"On one side, the A. Lincoln Wax Museum was a wonderful experience. On the other, it was a heart-breaking experience," Geving says in retrospect. "Although I didn't have a long time to look at our guest register, some of the notes written inside stick with me. From the first day, people came through saying what a good experience it was for their kids. That was important to me. The other thing that stands out in my mind is how proud my dad was on opening day. My dad reminds me of what Lincoln must have been like: quiet, very strong. He doesn't say anything unless he has something to say. For him, working on the museum was really one of the highlights of his life."

On April 11, 1865, Abraham Lincoln—in his last public address—said, "Important principles may and must be inflexible." Artists, historically, have well understood this statement. As conceived and completed by Hank Geving, the A. Lincoln Wax Museum incorporated this maxim into its mix, only to find—perhaps inevitably—that all men are not Abraham Lincoln. Springfield, Illinois, will never want for a sense of romance. But it will continue to miss one carefully crafted character. And the shape of a stovepipe crisp, stubborn and tall that refused—under every circumstance—to mildly melt away.

Opposite, top: A. Lincoln Wax Museum dioramas included one in which Lincoln appeared as a boy—and Hank Geving's father appeared as Thomas Lincoln. Opposite, bottom: Pick your president. While Lincoln pens the Emancipation Proclamation, Zachary Taylor sits in as a telegrapher.

Right: St. Louis Juke Box King Carl Trippe stands right of a Rock-Ola.

Below: The troops at Trippe's Ideal Novelty Company—the amusement empire that brought the giggles to Chain of Rocks Amusement Park.

Chain of Rocks Amusement Park & Fun Fair at Chain of Rocks Park

On day 29, Digger O'dell remains buried alive.

His premature interment wouldn't be half as harrowing if not for the raccoons that come nightly to ogle his prone and boxed body. Down from the north of St. Louis they creep to slip hungry looks through the holes in his coffin left by missing bricks. Often at night, Digger awakens to find the raccoons already there, rubbing their paws in ratty imitation of Peter Lorre. At such times, Digger reminds himself to breathe. His body reflexively tries to rise, and only the inevitable crack on his noggin bids him lie down again to play dead.

At present, daylight persists. Gazing upward and through the glass that rests mere inches from his face, Digger can see the underside of the canopy raised to keep rain off his tomb. He hears the clop of human feet and, seconds later, finds a face sticky with licorice peering downward and in, gawking, gaping and getting its ticket's worth. Words warble to Digger through a two-way speaker, but he can't understand this kid's question: The little snot's got a craw full of caramel corn.

Digger O'dell lets his eyelids droop closed like two vaudeville curtains. Endurance is the name of this amusement game, and he'll remain entombed until time expires—no matter what form of rodent pokes in its candied nose. In his stuffy, stone darkness, Digger monitors the pulse of the park. He considers the hum of the Swooper, the whine of the Whip and, ultimately, the gathering rumble of his own gawky snores. And precisely before he drowns in the shallows of sleep, the noises of this world blend into one lullaby. Life becomes a moon rocket ride borne over popcorn skies, and the faint tinkle of traffic far below plinks out xylophone notes on the ribbing of the Chain of Rocks Bridge.

owhere along Route 66 did the appearance of an amusement park seem more natural than at the western terminus of Chain of Rocks Bridge. The 1929 toll and truss bridge—built with a 45 degree bend in its middle—ricocheted cars across the Mississippi and spilled them out squealing over Riverview Drive. On the bluff above, Chain of Rocks Amusement Park simply sustained the carnival mood—winking hundreds of enticing eyes, scratching the stars with mechanical fingers, sticking out a tongue bumpy with carousel horses to suck squirming drivers inside.

The perky park that would survive half a century sprang from a city's quest to find clean water. By the 1840s, St. Louis suffered severe drinking problems:

Chouteau's Pond sat polluted with runoff from homes, slaughterhouses and waste from the Collier Lead Company, and the Mississippi itself was much too tainted to haul home by the bucketful. In 1872, the city opened Bissell's Point Waterworks four miles north of city center. By 1886, urban thirst had overwhelmed it, and construction was authorized for a northern extension—at Chain of Rocks.

Chain of Rocks Waterworks ended St. Louis' water supply problems, but did nothing to improve aesthetics inside the average glass. Drawn water settled in basins before taking the pipes into town—a process that removed sediment, but left water a weak shade of brown. In 1888, the *St. Louis Globe-Democrat* urged citizens not to drink in the dark after an eel appeared in a downtown sink. In 1895, the Health Commissioner called puny organisms visible in the water a breed of miniature crab. St. Louisans stomached the incidental seafood, but the metropolis cringed when Mayor David R. Francis succeeded in slating St. Louis as the site of the 1904 World's Fair. No one wanted the world to find a crawfish in its cup.

In 1901, the Municipal Assembly authorized the appointment of three hydraulic engineers to clear the water. The trio waded upriver and discovered that Quincy, Illinois, purified its water with iron and milk of lime. Two weeks before the Fair, the taps of St. Louis ran clear. Chain of Rocks Waterworks became a place of wonder.

In 1918, the city created Chain of Rocks Park on the bluff overlooking the waterworks. The 40-acre park sprouted fountains and goldfish ponds. Seven varieties of roses lined pathways, and the words CHAIN OF ROCKS bloomed in large, flowery letters. By 1927, the festive air around the water-works hung thick enough to attract ambitious eyes. On property adjacent to the park, a bouncing, baby amusement park was born.

The maiden seasons of Chain of Rocks Amusement Park lie shrouded in history. Certainty says only that Christian Hoffman served as early park president, hammering the Whip, the Dodgem Pavilion and a 1922 hand-carved carousel into place. Unique among the park's attractions stood the 1929 Swooper. The machine looked like a mechanical cold capsule. Only 19 were ever manufactured.

Hoffman was a man of thick accent and stubborn personality. Later park owners would refer to him as the Old German. At least one of those owners—Carl Trippe—thought little of Hoffman's style. Trippe was a former clerk for the Railway Express Company who in 1935 started the Ideal Novelty Company for phonographs, juke boxes and vending machines in St. Louis. In the early 1940s, Trippe contracted with Chain of Rocks Amusement Park to supply the machines in its penny arcade.

"Trippe pretty much had a lock on the pinball industry," explains Trippe's former son-in-law, Ralph Thole. "And a dispute arose between Trippe and the owner of Chain of Rocks Amusement Park. The owner told Trippe to take his machines and get out. Well, Trippe was pretty well-connected. He was so mad, he bought up all the park stock he could find and told Hoffman to get out."

Trippe shamed Hoffman's modest food stands by building the Sky Garden Bar and Restaurant. The elegant eatery offered breathtaking views of the mighty Mississip—including shots seen through magnifying machines for those who would step outside and insert a coin. Original paintings of riverside scenes graced the restaurant's walls. Trippe himself kept court in an upstairs office. An adjoining apartment provided living space for family at busy times of the year.

During his tenure at Chain of Rocks Amusement Park, Trippe received praise for his community involvement. In 1944, he staged the county fair at

Early day eateries at Chain of Rocks Park.

Trippe's Chain of Rocks Amusement Park was dominated by the Comet, a roller coaster that was scarier than most riders realized. "The Comet's nails were always coming loose," says Trippe's son-in-law, Ralph Thole. "Every Sunday I'd walk the Comet with a hammer and drive down the spikes that, through vibration, had worked their way up through the wooden framework that held down the tracks. We'd slam 'em once, and they'd go back in."

Emerson Electric Company, offering revelers a Ferris wheel, merry-go-round and a horse show. Annually, Trippe sponsored the Ozark AAU Junior Swimming Meet at the Chain of Rocks Amusement Park pool. The year before he died, Trippe established an Easter Egg Hunt at Chain of Rocks Amusement Park—an annual extravaganza that rolled on after his death.

In January of 1955, Carl Trippe suffered a fatal heart attack in his office at the Ideal Novelty Company. By 1958, his wife, Margaret, sought to sell Chain of Rocks Amusement Park. She approached William Zimmerman and Ken Thone—a pair of brothers-in-law operating Holiday Hill Amusement Park at Natural Bridge and Brown Roads in St. Louis. Zimmerman owned Holiday Hill. He had previously owned a golf range. Thone was a former auto repairman, a former jewelry repairman and a former Navy tugboat captain who managed Holiday Hill Amusement Park for Zimmerman. Both men liked Margaret Trippe's offer. Zimmerman bought Chain of Rocks Amusement Park; Thone

went to run it. The Trippe family gave the two a 99-year lease on the property.

On the advice of a veteran roller coaster man, Thone and Zimmerman tore down the wooden Comet. Frayed cables and bad decking doomed an old sky ride; bandstands vanished, and the swimming pool was suited with new bath houses. And although Thone and Zimmerman retained the Haunted Cave, the Mad House, the Dodgem Pavilion, the Rocket, the Whip, the 1922 carousel and the quirky Swooper, they turned Trippe's roller rink into an indoor miniature golf course. As a final means of making a fresh start, Thone and Zimmerman renamed the amusement complex. They called it Fun Fair at Chain of Rocks Park.

At Holiday Hill, the surest money came at season's start with the contracting of school picnics. Fun Fair at Chain of Rocks Park aggressively courted these outings. In the early 1960s, Thone and Zimmerman enlarged the park and hired a carnival operator from Florida to supply additional rides for the school picnic season.

Two rides that were perennial Fun Fair favorites—the 1922 hand-carved carousel and the delightful and quirky Swooper.

"Deggler Amusements brought in rides we normally wouldn't have because of the cost," says Ken Thone's son, Greg. "They were portable, trailer-mounted rides, and they could be set up and taken down in a day's time. They'd stay from the second week in April to the first or second week in June." During this first stretch of the season, Thone retained 150 to 200 employees. Afterward, he whittled personnel down to a skeleton crew.

Like Carl Trippe, Thone kept his office above the Sky Garden Bar and Restaurant. His guard dog, Sultan, policed the park at night but slept by day under his desk. Visitors entering Thone's inner sanctum found a man bursting with ideas and an office desk that growled without provocation. In later years, Sultan's pup, Satan, pulled office duty and patrolled the silent park after closing.

"We employed all kinds of strange people," says Greg Thone. "No bearded women or anything like that, but old carnival people. Everybody had a story. We had one guy who did odd jobs who was an ex-prize fighter. He fought in 48 bare-knuckle prize fights, won 24 and lost 24, but he was never knocked out. Our head maintenance man and his wife came from Russia during World War II; they were refugees. They had been sponsored by Trippe. When we bought the park, we kind of inherited them."

Sometimes, Trippe's sense of the absurd proved difficult for Thone to top. Trippe had once displayed a petrified mummy on his midway. Thone fired his best circus shot when he hired Digger O'dell—a fellow known for quirky feats of endurance.

"Digger O'dell was his stage name," says Greg Thone. "I don't remember where he came from, but I had heard that he sat on top of billboards and did crazy stunts for extended lengths of time.

"We buried Digger in a concrete-block coffin. The coffin was about 36 inches tall and eight feet long and three feet wide. It was equipped with an air conditioner and a tank that served as a toilet, and it sat on top of a concrete pad. We built a covering over it to keep the rain off.

"People paid to walk up and look at Digger through glass in the coffin's top. We had a microphone run to Digger so he could talk. People always thought he came out at night, but old Digger stayed in there 24 hours a day seven days a week for 30 or 33 days. We had left a few half blocks out on the coffin's side so you could pass him food. Digger always said at night the raccoons would come up there and look inside and scare him. They'd wake him up."

Over time, Fun Fair's Olympic-sized swimming pool became a financial drain. Thone joined forces with a local radio station, and together they created poolside Splash Parties. The raucous, wet concerts quickly became regular events.

"We held Splash Parties on Tuesday nights from seven to ten o'clock," explains Greg Thone. "The station would send a disc jockey, and a local rock-and-roll band would play. We brought in Paul Revere and the Raiders, and Ike and Tina Turner before they became famous." So popular did Splash Parties grow that they came to financially carry the park during the second half of its season.

Business at Fun Fair grew consistently through the 1960s, hitting a carnival high in the summer of 1970. The next year, Six Flags Over Mid-America opened in nearby Eureka and cut out the park's candied heart.

Ken Thone first noticed teenagers trickling away, enticed by the new park's single admission price.

"As soon as Six Flags opened in 1971, we knew we couldn't make a go of it much longer," he told a St. Louis paper years later. "Our northern location was a problem. We were losing school picnics. Teenagers weren't interested anymore in coming to a small park like ours which was always for the whole family. We had a picnic and barbeque area right outside the entrance which always brought the whole family out. That's not appealing to teenagers today who don't want to be where their parents are."

In 1973, a fire at Fun Fair destroyed Thone's office and the Sky Garden Bar and Restaurant. Two years later, Holiday Hill closed when its site was acquired by Lambert Field for airport parking expansion. Fun Fair absorbed the dead park's contraptions—including an Octopus, a Skydiver, electric cars, a ferris wheel and an army of toy tanks.

By the fall of 1976, Fun Fair was reeling under an imposed 9 1/2% tax—the sum of the city's 5% amusement tax and a 4 1/2% combined sales tax. Thone kept the rides assembled that winter for potential buyers to view. The following June, fire again ripped through Fun Fair at Chain of Rocks Park, destroying the dodgem cars and the 1922 hand-carved carousel. Disheartened and angry, Thone and Zimmerman closed Fun Fair for good on Labor Day of 1977. St. Louis became the first major city in the United States without its own amusement park. And the longest-lived play place on Route 66 existed no more.

On Wednesday, July 12, 1978, the auctioneers came to Fun Fair Park and offered up its pieces to a greatly indifferent crowd. The 1929 Swooper sold for a paltry $1,500. Scavengers carted away Perfumatics and plastic palm trees like old and brittle bones. No one could find any comfort in the situation—not even the raccoons, who took one last look at the carnage and crawled away lonely in search of Digger O'dell.

A bevy of the cutest little baby faces: Hilliard's Character Dolls

Hilliard's Character Dolls

Three shifts from civilization, and out where speed turns streets to silly putty, faces bounce by like rubber baby buggy bumpers. Features make poor impressions at umpteen miles an hour. Ear, nose and throat adopt the sharpness of pencil erasers.

Which may take tiny steps toward explaining the hobby of Margie Hilliard. The wife of Leslie Hilliard, and co-owner and operator of Hilliard Restaurant and Motel, Margie surrounded herself with button-eyed faces of the most immobile kind.

"Margie collected dolls," Gerry Linhardt offers in plastic understatement. "And her collection grew quite large. People stopped just to see these dolls all over a restaurant."

Margie's collection of porcelain heads drew goo-goo eyes five miles west of St. Clair, Missouri. There, Hilliard Restaurant and Motel huddled atop a modest hill—a two-building enterprise snagging traffic with a simple, plywood sign. While Leslie checked flesh-and-blood patrons into motel rooms, Margie spent her days in the restaurant, frying the chicken for which she was famous and dressing her bisque-porcelain brood.

"Most of Margie's dolls were displayed around a central column," explains old Hilliard neighbor, Edie Woodcock. "I don't know if it was a support column, but you could see the dolls from all sides."

Hilliard's Restaurant, like most of the road's hash heavens, was an unassuming building. No counter served customers. Diners gathered around four-person tables under bulbs meekly lit. If the eatery printed slick menus, no one remembers them. But they do remember the infants that seemed to crawl unchecked from every nook and cranny.

Margie acquired most of her dolls from sources overseas. They were dolls aimed squarely at the serious collector. Many came complete with preposterous price tags stuck to their dainty, dimpled bottoms. In Margie's collection, French Bru dolls smiled famous Bru smiles. Dutch dolls wore wooden shoes. Elegant china gave arms and legs shape.

Sometime after letting their restaurant and motel out of the cradle, Margie and Leslie realized the power of their cafe's dolly draw. Images of the dolls began gracing postcards. Margie began offering dolls for sale. She maintained a show place near the highway's edge—an area in which she also offered bedspreads and flower pots cemented with tiny, colored stones. The slightly plump Margie became quite shrewd when selling dolls. She often demanded prices that could make the biggest kids cry.

"Margie was very knowledgeable about her dolls' worth," says Gerry Linhardt. "When I was a child, my family often visited Leslie and Margie. We children never played with those dolls. Maybe we wanted to, but we knew we dared not. It was just something children didn't do."

Although Margie's collection was a child's dream, the Hilliard's never had children of their own. Today, scattered nieces and nephews remember the collection of dolls that made a restaurant famous. The bypassing of Route 66 proved particularly cruel to the Hilliard businesses, demanding drivers exit the new highway and backtrack a substantial distance to reach them. Leslie Hilliard died in July of 1976. After Margie's death in April of 1988, the dolls were sold at auction. Today, nothing remains of Hilliard's Character Dolls but vague, crawling memories. And a fog of faces screaming past at 70 miles an hour—blunted by speed-induced indifference.

Earl Woodcock stands at the fireplace built by his uncle of Ozark Rock Curios stones.

Ozark Rock Curios

In a darkness sticky as a Tallahassee napkin, the Fluorescent House prepares to swallow another victim. Oak walls smother sound, and humidity hugs the tin roof like a thing with tentacles. But a flip of a switch, and the air begins to buzz in increasing, peaceful plum. Ultraviolet pulsates from the center of bruised bulbs, and the buried, the exhumed and the carefully arranged specimens appear ready for inspection.

In this magenta light, Mother Nature dons carnival clothes. Stones glow like moonrock or nuggets of key lime. Minerals drip lipstick, and boulders rouge their bottoms like old grannies with bad aim. So striking sits this rock show, that it takes attendees time to notice something at room's rear. Something with sharp eyes and red toenails. Something that moves.

And at that geological second, the screams could split the hills.

As a creature of the American curbside, the curio will never make an endangered species list. Artful, artless, costly or cheap—the trinket is a treasure Americans keep close to their hearts. Proof positive one has traveled—and stopped to shop awhile.

On America's highways, the creation of the curio business came after the establishment of essential roadside concessions. In the beginning, the gas station, the cafe and the tourist camp pumped, poured and slung bath towels at wandering souls. Only when ashtrays—and other bits of bric-a-brac—failed to remain with their owners did someone think of selling travelers a formal souvenir. The first keepsake dealers were themselves often surprised to find they stood knee-deep in doodads.

"Dad couldn't find a job," explains Missouri's Earl Woodcock. "He finally found work helping an old miner dig blue tiff near a little town called Anaconda. Blue tiff is a rare rock. The old miner went broke, and couldn't pay Dad, so he gave him some blue tiff and told him, 'Set these rocks in front of your home on the highway. They'll sell, and you'll get your money.' That's what Dad done."

The souvenir empire that became Ozark Rock Curios started on the smallest of scales. Paul Jacob Woodcock was a Nazarene minister. In 1931, he moved from Iowa to Roby, Missouri, with his wife, Lola May, and his parents. In 1932, he took a large leap northeast and landed on Route 66 near St. Clair, Missouri. A tangle with a tightfisted miner taught Paul common rocks could sell. He began making trips to nearby Potosi and Richwoods, pulling sponge rock and chert from clumps of red clay and selling the stones to tourists traveling past his door.

Lola May and Paul Jacob Woodcock.

Paul found an early customer in Meramec Caverns. The newborn show cave sought stalactites to sell as souvenirs. Paul mined the treasures out of smaller, local caves and sold them wholesale to Meramec Caverns king Lester B. Dill. Two of the largest stalactites Paul mined—including one weighing more than 1000 pounds—for years graced the grounds of Ozark Rock Curios, serving as informal landmarks and symbols of quality to discerning rock hounds.

Between two stony pillars, Paul erected an Ozark Rock Curios marquee. He suspended stone birdhouses and planters from sign's bottom, and constructed rock stands to display minerals in the raw. As a rule, the more expensive the specimen, the higher it sat on Paul's shelves.

Shoppers found rocky windmills and tombstones standing against a novelty shed. The shed housed gazing globes and flower pots freckled with pebbles. Good-natured scares could be got in the nearby Fluorescent House.

"The Fluorescent House was just a little, old square building," Earl Woodcock remembers. "It was pitch dark, and we filled it with rocks that would change color under an ultraviolet light. Remember those little balsam wood turtles? The kind that moved their feet and head when the wind blew? Well, Dad had some of those in there with red eyes made out of crushed rock, and they had their toes all painted. There was an exhaust fan in the Fluorescent House because it was hot in there in the summer. I'd take folks inside, flip that exhaust fan on, and I'd get people as close to that turtle as I could. Then I'd hit it with that ultraviolet light. They'd see that thing setting there and moving, and you ought to hear the screaming.

"I waited on customers from the time I was big enough to talk," Earl continues. "I used to get more tips because I was little, and I knew the name of every stone out there, and some of them are hard to say when you're small. My brothers and I got paid for breaking rocks. Many times we'd get up early in the morning and go down to the lower lot—the wholesale lot—and take big rocks and break them into pieces. At the end of the week, Dad would ask us, 'How much work did you do?' He'd write it down in the book, and, when school started, he'd give us a Montgomery Wards catalogue. We'd pick out our school clothes, and Dad would deduct what he owed us from that. If we wanted money for something we saw on the road, he did the same thing."

In the later 1930s, Ozark Rock Curios installed Phillips 66 gasoline pumps. Around the same time, Paul's wholesale business took a mobile turn. Photos dating from 1938 show Paul and family slinging sponge rock into a St. Clair boxcar bound for customers back east. Big buyers received rocks by rail in New York and Grand Rapids, Michigan. Others customers saw Paul delivering the stony goods in person—on one of countless trading trips he took around the country.

"Dad started mining Missouri rock to take to other states," Earl explains. "He'd drive to Illinois, trade for Illinois rock; go to Michigan, trade for Michigan rock. He ran all over the United States in an old Model A flatbed pickup truck with a one-and-a-half ton camper box on the back, and he lived on the road for weeks or months at a time." Paul's trips eventually took him through every state in the Union. On occasion, he returned home with his truck weighed down by ores from Canada and Mexico. In Arizona, Paul scooped his own wood out of the Petrified Forest; in Illinois, he found his own fossil ferns in local coal dumps.

Paul routinely departed St. Clair with a truckload of curios fashioned by his wife, Lola May. Lola crafted her keepsakes with a keen artist's eye and an instinct that told her what tourists wanted. She crafted curios by the thousands. Lola's output hit an assembly-line high after Ozark Curios moved to new quarters and she enjoyed a large basement in which to work.

"Mom had metal pans like cake pans," explains Earl. "Each pan held a different type of rock, and each pan was fixed to a bicycle wheel that Dad had mounted to a board. Mom would set a piece of wax paper on the end of an apple box. She would have colored concrete mixed—red, green, blue or yellow—and she would trowel this concrete over, say, a number of vases. Then she'd turn this wheel and take some of this rock or some of that rock, and push the stones into the concrete.

"Dad had big shelves downstairs. Mom would slide her finished curios onto these. When we kids came home from school, we'd pull whatever Mom had made off the wax paper and restack the boards. We'd save the wax paper because Mom used it over. When Dad wanted to go somewhere, we'd wrap the curios in newspaper and pack 'em in apple boxes."

In the later 1940s, the state of Missouri enlarged St. Clair's stretch of Route 66. Paul and family found their business buried under new eastbound lanes, and moved Ozark Rock Curios one-quarter mile west. The relocated Ozark Rock Curios never offered gasoline, and the business forevermore lacked the towering pillars that had stood on either side of the Ozark Rock Curios sign. In 1948, Paul built a new house on the property—pouring electrical wires into enduring concrete. "Before the state come through a second time and took more property, there was another little house out here that was the original farmhouse," says Earl Woodcock. "Grandma Woodcock lived in it. She'd take off walking down the old highway, using an umbrella with a long spike on it as a cane. You could here her going for miles: click, click, click. She'd walk all the way to Anaconda. And she'd call on people. Get 'em to go to church."

Religion remained a Woodcock family cornerstone. As a Nazarene minister, Paul frequently preached in St. Clair on Sunday nights. After Ozark Rock Curios moved to its new location, the Woodcocks attended church in Stanton. On Sunday mornings, Paul routinely drove his new truck down backroads to pick up parishioners in need of a lift. Riders entered the truck's back via a steel ladder. Inside, they found a bench and a small wood-burning stove that offered warm comfort on cooler mornings.

Throughout the 1950s and into the 1960s, business at Ozark Rock Curios boomed. In 1962, Paul's brother Dave gathered together a number of remarkable rocks. He fashioned the stones into a one-of-a-kind fireplace inside Paul's house. The hearty hearth might have warmed Woodcock family members forever if Paul hadn't taken a good look at himself one day—and heard a Higher Calling.

"Dad went to Albuquerque to preach to the Indians," says Earl. "He sold the house in 1963.

"He'd gotten arthritis real bad—Dad drank milk and Wheaties on the road all the time, and he had so much calcium in his system that it got behind his eyes. He finally decided to go out west and quit, although he did keep his wholesale business after he moved out there. The last few years Ozark Rock Curios was in business, Dad mined petrified wood with a bulldozer. He shipped it by train all over the United States."

Paul and Lola May set up house on the Navajo Reservation. Lola learned silver-smithing from the Navajos, and Paul spent his free time driving loads of rock to Michigan. Paul's last trading trip took him back to Grand Rapids. "He lost his memory in Grand Rapids," explains Earl's wife, Edie Woodcock. "He sat on the side of the highway for three days. When the police opened the door of his truck, here was this little, old, unshaven man with a big grin on his face because somebody found him."

Ozark Rock Curios closed in July of 1977.

Earl and Edie Woodcock continue to live in the house Paul Jacob Woodcock built in 1948—on the grounds of Ozark Rock Curios' second location. In 1995, and after 32 years, Earl and Edie bought the house back into their family. They found the stone fireplace constructed by Paul's brother Dave standing virtually unscathed.

"This is what they call ironwood, and this is flourite from Illinois," Earl points out, standing on that hearth and sharing rocky memories. "This is feldspar—what they got the color from for your false teeth years ago. This is white lead. They used to put it in women's face powder, ground up snow white. Years ago, if you picked up a can of face powder, it was real heavy. And yet lead today is called a killer. These gals were working on their faces years ago, and they all lived to be 80 or 90."

On shelves and dashboards across America, modern curios live long lives, too, thanks to factories that pump out fuzzy dice and plastic glow-light Madonnas. But along Route 66, the early trinket makers put pieces of themselves into every souvenir they sold. Dust off one of these pieces, and you'll still see shiny bits of personality and care. Those are the qualities that turned trinkets into treasures and buys into bargains so many years ago.

A SOUVENIR EMPIRE EVOLVES

Above: The first home of Ozark Rock Curios—a novelty shed and a yard filled with tombstones and birdhouses.

Above, left: Paul Woodcock's two prize stalactites. Earl Woodcock remembers spending afternoons sitting atop them as a child. They sold to the Grotto of the Redemption in West Bend, Iowa. They stand there today.

Left: In 1938, the Woodcock family loads sponge rock into a St. Clair boxcar bound for points east.

Below: An Ozark Rock Curios postcard shows the business expanding. Note the additional rock stands and the Phillip's 66 gas pumps. In time, Ozark Rock Curios boasted ten rock stands. The stands were arranged by ascending price with the first offering rocks at ten cents apiece and the last holding stones that cost hundreds of dollars. The old Fluorescent House would be the final structure standing on this spot—torn down by the Woodcock family in the later 1990's.

Above: A spread of rocky trinkets.

Right: Ozark Rock Curios' second truck. The trailer provided living space during collecting trips.

Below: Dave Woodcock and pup near the new Ozark Rock Curios sign. The pillars of the original sign crumbled when Paul attempted to move them.

Below, right: The last location of Ozark Rock Curios in Missouri. Paul Woodcock built the house in 1948. Today, Paul's son and daughter-in-law call it home.

The Snake Man at Silver Star Court. The name of his game was endurance—in the company of the coiled and quick.

The Snake Man at Silver Star Court

Since the day the first wiggler made his devilish debut in the Garden of Eden, the Snake's has been a shadow that has refused to slink away. Consider the stranglehold the Hisser holds on history: Hercules clubbing his hydra, Cleopatra clasping her asp, Rikki-Tikki-Tavi and Don't Tread on Me. The snake is both a symbol of healing and a thing to be whacked in the grass, the cause of King Arthur's defeat at Camlann and an honored dance partner of the Hopi Nation. The Snake is complicated. The Snake is our kin. He's the flashy uncle with bad teeth who comes to Christmas dinner and takes the turkey leg simply because he's always taken it. No one argues with him. No one's sure what might come out of his mouth.

Streaking down today's interstate, it's difficult to imagine the impact the words "Snake Pit" once carried brushed blood-red on billboards. In a day when pets meant puppies and kittens, and boa constrictors didn't lurk in the apartment across the hall, a meeting with the Snake still carried mythical connotations. In the American West, facing the Snake became a right of passage, a confirmation that far-off lands were being achieved, a reminder that all journeys were dabblings in danger and danger would—inevitably—one day lead to death. For centuries, people met the Devil on the road and jockeyed with him for favors. At snake pits, travelers could sip an orange soda while the Devil sat in a hole and wrestled with himself.

The hole that housed the Snake Man at Silver Star Court was scooped as an afterthought—an impromptu means to make money and distinguish one motel from others on the road. Situated seven and three-quarter miles west of St. Clair, Missouri, the Silver Star was owned and operated by Paul and Cora Smith. For years, the Silver Star found fame in its affordable cafe where hungry mouths could feast on seven burgers for a buck. Then, one day, the Snake Man came wiggling down the road.

"The Snake Man was traveling through," says St. Clair local, Edie Woodcock. "He was traveling on foot. He carried his snakes in a gunny sack."

The Silver Star Court: First a place to get a burger. And then a place to get a bite.

The Snake Man at the Silver Star Court remains a perfect example of one of the road's free and anonymous spirits. Strolling through this world, he knocked on doors, packing poison and a proposition. Odds say he originated with a circus or reptile show coiled near some beach-side boardwalk. But on Route 66, the Snake Man was his own ringmaster.

No record survives outlining the exact financial agreement struck between Paul Smith and the Snake Man. But eye-witnesses well-remember what Paul got for his money. "Paul Smith and the Snake Man dug a hole in the ground," says Edie Woodcock's husband, Earl. "They dug it in front of the motel. And the old boy stayed down there in that hole for 30 days at a time with the snakes. That was his act."

A hut was built over the Snake Man's earthy room. A quarter bought the curious a walk through this shelter and a peek at the daily practices of a man living in jeopardy. Often, visitors found the Snake Man animated—on his feet and ready to lecture. Sometimes they discovered him wrapped in his poison wards and passively paging through a book. A glass cover lay over the hole. The Snake Man was fond of picking up rattlers and squirting the underside of this glass with venom.

Simple needs could lead to occasions for dramatic showmanship. The Snake Man's meals were brought to him and carefully extended into his world. Baser physical needs were tended to during breaks from public peeping. The Snake Man told inquisitive guests that getting a good night's rest was his hardest trick to manage. In truth, the Snake Man crept into a hidden cubbyhole at night—and slept as soundly as a baby boa.

"He told me he'd been bit several times," says Earl Woodcock. "The way he'd grab those snakes up, it was no wonder. Some people just aren't afraid of snakes.

"My mother was there one day with me. The Snake Man was standing down in his pit, and he had the top open. My mother was quite a cut-up, and she was laughing about something. The Snake Man had a big old python down there. He lifted it up, and he said, 'Here, Mom, take this!' And Mom took that python and carried it around and laughed about it. It didn't bother her a bit. The other people watching that day thought that was pretty neat."

The Snake Man's association with Silver Star Court lasted several seasons. During that time, he was seldom seen above ground. One day, after many slithering sunsets, the Snake Man at Silver Star Court vanished into the venomous horizon from whence he came. Cora Smith—who as a rule brought him breakfast—entered the small hut one morning to find the pit empty and the Snake Man gone. He'd given no hint of his intention to leave. But he had taken the time to pluck up and take with him every one of his poisonous pets. For this last favor, Cora Smith was grateful.

In the 1970s, the Silver Star Court succumbed to the wrecking ball. Well before that time, the roadside snake pit had hollowed out a permanent hole in the American psyche. Nowadays, folks who never saw a roadside snake pit remember them as shoddy establishments run by swindlers with cold-blooded hearts. Admittedly, bad apples fall from every tree. But the Snake himself would tell you he had his share of caring partners along old Highway 66. And a good word or two is in order for the best of these who—at risk to themselves—so skillfully gave us the shivers.

Opposite: By the time westbound travelers reached the Snake Man at Silver Star Court, those that had motored all the way from Chicago had driven almost four hundred miles dotted with Meramec Caverns barns. A smattering of the painted advertisements today survive along the route and stand among the road's most beloved icons.

The wonderful world of Meramec Caverns. Top: The Jungle Room—perhaps the last collection of colored cave lights on all of Route 66. Bottom: Loot Rock, where Frank and Jesse reportedly divided dirty dough.

Meramec Caverns & Fisher's Cave

f King Kong ever turns in his bananas and retires, chances are he'll buy one very large motor home and putter straight toward Missouri's Meramec Caverns. The gargantuan attraction, located on the shores of the stony Meramec River, stands head and hoary shoulders above all others on the road.

Here, big is as big does, and the caverns have meant serious business since 1720 when French explorer Jacques Renault dipped his tootsies into the crystal rich dust of their innards—and found saltpeter. Glutted with this explosive ingredient, Salt Peter Cave—as the caverns were first called—supplied boom powder for umpteen French and Indian skirmishes as well as the formal War Between the States. Legend says Jesse James—and his Confederate brother Frank—rode with Quantrill's Irregulars in the Civil War's last days and beat the powder mill back into the dust from whence it came.

Peace and milder pastimes found Salt Peter Cave in the Gay '90s. When once upon a sweaty Saturday revelers found the dance hall in Stanton too warm to waltz, the crowd spilled down to Salt Peter Cave and helped kick up a craze for cave dances that swelled well into the next century. Soon Salt Peter Cave's subterranean Ballroom boasted a wooden dance floor, a bar and its own flock of fiddlers. In the summer of 1901, an ax-wielding group of square dancers smacked a hole in a cave wall and went on to discover the cave's

An early-day dance inside Meramec Caverns' Ballroom.

upper levels. The stage was set for the arrival of Lester B. Dill.

Lester B. Dill was a natural born cave-man—a metamorphic entrepreneur with no carnival experience—only an enduring affection for this earth's dirt. Born in St. Louis on November 28, 1898, Dill was the second child of nine born to Thomas Benton and Daisy Crockett Dill. As an infant, he moved with his family to his father's boyhood stomping grounds at the bottomlands of the Meramec River. At ten years of age, he filled time between farm chores leading St. Louis thrill seekers through nearby Fisher's Cave.

Adulthood for Dill meant army duty, marriage to Mary Hamby and an eight-year odyssey that began in 1920. He slipped through Oklahoma's oil boom and Florida's real estate grab before returning to St. Louis as a carpenter. In 1926, the state of Missouri began purchasing property for what would become Meramec State Park. An initial 5,778 acres were stitched together—including land that contained Fisher's and Mushroom Caves. In the spring of 1927, Dill's father became Park Superintendent. Lester himself negotiated a lease with state officials to commercialize Fisher's and Mushroom Caves.

Dill raised restrooms from scrap lumber. He stocked makeshift souvenir stands with homemade trinkets. State park regulations limited his ability to advertise, so Dill took promotion where he found it.

When once a visitor discovered a square nail on the floor of Fisher's Cave, Dill proclaimed the peg a remnant of a dance floor built for the 1865 inaugural ball of Governor Thomas C. Fletcher. Word reached the St. Louis papers. For a time, folks came to Fisher's Cave simply to seek square nails.

In the early 1930s, Meramec State Park expanded. Dill lost his cave concession. He shopped for a new cave to commercialize. On May 1, 1933, he signed a five-year lease with an option to buy Salt Peter Cave from owner Charley Rueppele. Dill changed the cave's name to Meramec Caverns. He enlisted a local sawmill crew to construct a road to his attraction. Time prohibited the creation of a parking lot, so Dill gamely graded the road into his cave's mouth and dubbed Meramec Caverns the "World's First Drive-In Cave." He armed his children with bumper signs and set them loose on every car that rolled through the door.

Meramec Caverns opened on Decoration Day of 1933. For a fee of 40 cents, first-day visitors were obliged to haul themselves by rope up the incline to the Wine Room. One restroom served ladies exclusively. Gentlemen were sent to a sycamore tree.

"When I first came here, we had one string of lights going down the center of the corridor and hanging on a piece of wire," says long-time Meramec Caverns employee, Jim Gauer. "In the Theatre Room, we had a long pole with a hundred watt light bulb on it. You plugged it into a socket and showed the Stage Curtains that way."

Believing subterranean sock hops could keep his enterprise alive, Dill resurrected Meramec Caverns' Ballroom. In 1934, he sold half interest in Meramec Caverns to his old high school chum Vivian "Pete" Peterson. Charley Rueppele died, and Dill and Peterson bought Meramec Caverns. In the thin days that followed, Pete moved onto the property to live in a tent. His tool-filled jalopy became Meramec Cavern's mobile machine shop and road repair kit. Dill sank what money he could muster into highway billboards—and the broad sides of barns.

"The idea to paint the name Meramec Caverns on barns began in the 1930s," says Jim Gauer. "Mr. Dill and his wife went to Florida on vacation. They saw an ad for Lookout Mountain painted on a barn.

Mr. Dill said, 'I think we can do that.' At first, the barns were just white letters on a black background. Years later, we changed them all to red and yellow emblems because you can see them better."

Adds Les Turilli, Jr., "My great-grandfather also painted birdhouses. He put them on fence posts along the highway. People would see these things every couple hundred yards. They'd slow down to look at a birdhouse, and in little letters it would say, 'Come to Meramec Caverns!'"

In August of 1935, Dill hired a plumber to dry out the Ballroom's dance floor with a gas torch. The feed line snapped, and a wall of fire blew beneath Dill's knees. Dill spent six months recuperating in a veterans hospital. Days on his back gave him ample time to think, and he thought of Meramec Caverns. In subsequent years, Dill's underground promotional schemes would hit new heights.

Following World War II, Dill played off a public preoccupied with the drop of the Atomic Bomb. He declared Meramec Caverns the "World's First Atomic Refuge," created a Bomb Shelter Passage and stocked it with rations and thousands of gallons of water. Visitors paid to see this haven prepared as "a modern Noah's Ark." As an apocalyptic incentive to come again, patrons were given tiny cards with their admission tickets—cards that insured them they had room reserved inside the fallout shelter in the event the Big One dropped.

In December of 1941, Dill, Professor of Geology J. Harlen Bretz and two University of Chicago students drained water from a sitting pond inside Meramec Caverns and went on to discover an underground river passage beyond. Soon afterward, Dill announced the discovery of a strong box and other relics found inside this passage—items, he claimed, that could be traced by legal means to the hands of Jesse James. When the press reacted mildly, Dill waited a few years, stepped back and took another swing: In 1949, Dill and his son-in-law Rudy Turilli ostensibly produced the living and breathing Jesse James in the person of J. Frank Dalton. The notorious 100-year old outlaw, they said, had been living in Lawton, Oklahoma, under his new name. This time, the papers exploded, and the creation of Meramec Caverns stood famously complete.

"On average, one person per tour says they're related to Jesse James," says Meramec Caverns tour guide Travis Roach. "You have to laugh, because they all think they're telling you something new."

Meramec Caverns remains one of the few places in America adults can comfortably feel ten years old. Past the caverns' spinning entrance turnstiles—and a moonshiner's shack easily mistaken for a Jesse James hide-out—wonder tangibly trickles from all sides. Few places have over the years played so perfectly off popular culture. At a junction past the Gunpowder Room, a small hole huddles in a wall. Dubbed the Honeymoon Room, Dill turned the nook into television history in the 1960s when it appeared on NBC's *Art Linkletter Show.* For purposes of entertainment, Dill dressed a newlywed couple in leopard skins, confined them to the hole and promised them a free trip to the Bahamas if they could find a hidden key within ten days. Each time a cave tour passed, the Cro-Magnon couple were required to act out a skit. The humiliation—and the publicity—lasted the full ten days: Dill didn't hide the key until day ten.

Prehistoric promotion: The honeymooning cave couple.

Unlike nearby Onondaga and other state-run caves, Meramec Caverns continues to slick a portion of its insides with brightly-colored lights. The circus hues underscore the strangeness of formations and fuel the feeling of a wonderland grown mad. At Loot Rock, Frank and Jesse James split booty by the fire. A wax effigy of Lassie stands lonely and looking for Timmy at the Hollywood Connection.

"Lassie was given to us by the studio that filmed the TV series," explains tour guide Travis Roach. "In 1966, they came to Meramec Caverns and filmed an episode here. Unfortunately, our original Lassie floated away in the floods of 1982. The studio sent us a new one. The only problem with the new Lassie is it looks like a German shepherd."

So completely does Meramec Caverns' animated atmosphere swallow customers, that emotional reactions grow commonplace. Dill planned his tour's crescendo at the Stage Curtains—an enormous onyx waterfall over which lights splash and Kate Smith sings "God Bless America." The formation is dedicated to this country's fighting men and women. Veterans grow teary-eyed at the tribute. But so do the rest of us, overwhelmed by a feeling we've reached the center of the earth promised by Jules Verne and found it grandly patriotic.

One woman was so impressed with Meramec Caverns that she decided to make it the final resting place of her dearly departed husband.

"That happened several years ago," says Travis Roach. "Her husband had been cremated, and she had him in an urn. The tour got back to the Mirror River. The tour guide turned around, and there she was, dumping her husband's ashes into the river in the middle of a tour."

At present, no marker pays tribute to the spot where the underground fan took his last dip. But give Meramec Caverns time. Lester B. Dill, above and beyond any showman on the road, well understood the value of a good buildup. From barn roof to birdhouse, Jesse James to Jungle Room, the legacy Dill left is one of wonder unadulterated. No one as yet has risen to snatch that crown from Meramec Caverns.

Not even King Kong. Ask him while you both wait for the caverns' next tour.

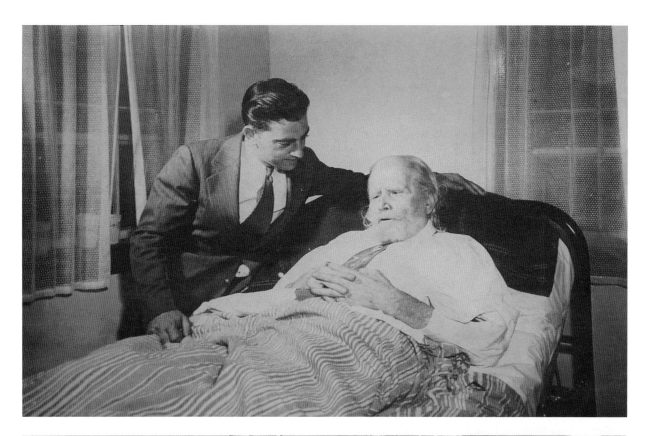

Top: Rudy Turilli attends the mysterious—and occasionally dangerous—J. Frank Dalton. Bottom: Jesse James Wax Museum guide Tammy Franklin with the ear that reportedly proves J. Frank Dalton was Jesse James.

Jesse James Wax Museum

n September 5, 1949, one of the strangest processions to oompah through the Ozarks took place at Meramec Caverns in Stanton, Missouri. Across the bald prairie of a parking lot, happy hands hefted a shrunken man on a stretcher and bore him toward a room filled with party cake and candles. The bed-ridden gentleman claimed to be celebrating his 102nd birthday. And, so he said, his name was Jesse James.

"We actually have film footage taken on the day J. Frank Dalton arrived," says Meramec Caverns Cave-King-To-Be, Les Turilli, Jr. "There were thousands of people in the parking lot. Everybody was waving and screaming his name."

Along the wagon trails of history, no wrangler holds a horse bun to Jesse Woodson James. His name stands bold and black and alone, a marquee-sized moniker anchored by the alliteration of two capitalized fishhooks and a reputation that scores savage on the cowpoke shoot-'em-up scale. Born in Centerville, Missouri, the lad who would ride with Quantrill's Irregulars during Civil War days—and subsequently cut a swath across America's financial institutions—remains an enigma—a combo of good and ghastly that can't mix but somehow does—a moral teeter-totter that tickles romantics and bullies small brains. On silver screens, Jesse invariably appears superhuman, flickering through everything from *Jesse James Meets Frankenstein's Daughter* to an episode of Rod Serling's *Twilight Zone.* No medium stands tall enough to corner him. Song, paint and poetry all reach for the skies.

Small wonder the grave itself has had trouble swallowing Jesse James. History has Jesse shot by Robert Ford on April 3, 1882—bushwhacked from

behind while straightening a wall hanging. But like Marilyn Monroe snoring her life away—or Elvis passing his last on the pooper—the official account of James' death proved too inglorious for many admirers to accept. By 1902, Jesse's body had been exhumed and reburied simply to ensure it was stiff. Half a century later, a dozen old men rode out of the woodwork—each calling the corpse counterfeit and each themselves claiming to be the authentic Jesse James. All had their turns at the microphone. One captured the confidence of a wide-eyed cave expert named Rudy Turilli.

"My grandfather was absolutely fascinated with Jesse James," says Les Turilli, Jr. "He researched Jesse for 23 years. When all the old guys were claiming to be Jesse James, he successfully discredited every one. Then he found Frank Dalton."

By 1948, Rudy Turilli had established himself as the Heir Eccentric at Missouri's Meramec Caverns. Newly related to caverns' owner and promotional Pooh-bah Lester B. Dill, Rudy had married Dill's oldest daughter, Francena, and shown his father-in-law that he could cut the commercial cave mustard.

"In the late 1940s, Rudy participated in a promotional stunt that made world news," says Les Turilli, Jr. "He and another fellow climbed the Empire State Building. They got on top in leopard-skin caveman suits, and they threatened to jump off unless every person in the world went to Meramec Caverns. The authorities finally talked them down. Rudy and his friend got thrown in jail for nine days, but the story made all the state papers."

When Frank Dalton's claim to the Jesse James name surfaced in Lawton, Turilli and Dill assumed Dalton to be another fraud. Yet neither could let the story lie. Meramec Caverns had an enormous interest in Jesse James. In 1941, Dill had learned of a legend that said the James-Younger Gang had holed up inside Meramec Caverns. One year later, a stash of stolen loot was discovered in a previously uncharted caverns passage—booty that included a strong box stolen off a James-robbed train. If the big boy of the bad hats still breathed, Dill and Turilli were going to find him.

Rudy rode to Oklahoma to meet Dalton. He became intrigued by what he found. The bedridden old man who claimed to be Missouri's meanest outlaw was smoothing the spurs off all skeptics. The press was putting its confidence in print, and no interviewer—however fast on the draw—could pop a hole in Dalton's story. Most interesting of all, this self-proclaimed Jesse had an alibi for his silence to date: Dalton explained that—on April 3, 1882—Robert Ford had actually shot Charles Bigelow, another James-Younger Gang member. Bigelow's brains had been blown out and buried under the James name so the genuine Jesse—i.e. Dalton—could live in peace. Missouri Governor T.T. Crittenden had been in on the ruse. Dalton and the rest of the gang had made a pact to disclose their true identities only after they reached the age of 100.

Crawling over Dalton with a magnifying glass, Rudy was astounded to discover damage done to the old man's body agreed with reports of injuries sustained by Jesse James—from a mutilated tip on a left-hand index finger, to evidence of severe burns on both feet, to a drooping right eyelid, to bullet scars along the left shoulder, hairline and abdomen. If Dalton wasn't Jesse James, he'd groomed himself head to heel with a potato peeler and a cheese knife. Arrangements were made to bring him to Stanton.

"J. Frank Dalton sent Mr. Turilli out to find other living gang members," recounts Jesse James Wax Museum tour guide, Tammy Franklin. "Mr. Turilli found John Tramell, the cook. Mr. Turilli told Tramell, 'Jesse James wants you to come down to Meramec Caverns for his 102nd birthday.' And the cook said, 'I don't know Jesse James.' So Mr. Turilli went back to Dalton, and Dalton told him, 'I didn't give you the password; that's why Tramell wouldn't come.' Mr. Turilli asked, 'Why didn't you give me the password?' And Dalton said, 'Because I wanted

to know if I could trust you, first.' So Dalton gave Mr. Turilli the password, and Mr. Turilli went back to John Tramell and brought the cook back for Jesse's birthday."

A photograph of the birthday festivities hangs today inside the Jesse James Wax Museum: Surrounded by onlookers, J. Frank Dalton reclines in a wheelchair with feet snuggled in pillows. John Tramell stands behind him. In the center of the room—and near wife Francena—Rudy Turilli gives a high sign. A banner wishes *Happy Birthday 102 Jesse James*. There's not a horse in the room, but by the looks of the cake on the table, the entire James Gang with Turilli's in tow could have escaped under cover of frosting if the sheriff had shown.

Dalton was quartered in a cottage on Meramec Caverns property. He drank heavily and—for a man who's favorite hymn was reportedly "What a Friend We Have in Jesus"—minced no words when angry. "He was friendly other than with the reporters," says Meramec Caverns barn-painter, Jim Gauer. "The reporters were there night and day bothering him, and he asked for a six-shooter. They gave him a six-shooter, and he actually shot holes through the ceiling to keep them fellas out. The folks here got to worrying he might kill somebody, so they started taking the powder out of the bullets and replacing the lead. That didn't work, because he could pick those bullets up and say, 'Something's wrong with these.' He knew the weight of a proper bullet."

While Dalton was busy murdering his ceiling, Rudy Turilli was fighting the good fight for legitimacy. Over the years, his faith in Dalton led him to appearances on *What's My Line?* and *The Tonight Show*. Rudy's face peppered paper after paper, offering $10,000 to anyone who could prove Dalton a fraud. The publicity rained silver over Meramec Caverns. The research led Turilli to found his own Dalton tribute in the form of the Jesse James Wax Museum.

Today, the museum stands on a shot-up shoulder of Route 66 near Stanton, Missouri. Inside, life-sized figures of Frank Dalton, Rudy Turilli, Cole Younger and others scowl and conspire. Firearms that purportedly belonged to James-Younger Gang members are uncovered and cocked by tour guides.

A waxen J. Frank Dalton greets visitors inside the Jesse James Wax Museum.

A James family tree crawls over one wall. Antique curiosities lay low and age—from Frank James' bathtub to the barber chair in which Jesse took his last trim.

Over all, there exists a gleefully gruesome accent on body parts. A photo of gang member Charley Pitts' riddled torso compliments official James autopsy pictures. Arrows poke at bullet holes. Jesse's wax mom stands without the arm she lost in a bomb blast. There are computer-enhanced aging projections that turn a 34-year-old Jesse into a dumpy J. Frank Dalton, and a grotesque study in 12-inch ears that seeks to prove beyond a shadow of a Q-tip that Dalton's lobe was Jesse's own.

In the early 1950s, Rudy Turilli and Lester Dill petitioned the Franklin Country Circuit Court to change Dalton's name back to Jesse James. With hat in hand, Dalton was carried into the courthouse on a stretcher. Judge Ransom A. Breur, dancing more daintily than an Ito, made the official observation:

"There is no evidence here to show that this gentleman, if he ever was Jesse James, has ever changed his name. If his name has never been changed from Jesse James, he is still Jesse James in name, and there is nothing for this court to pass on. If he isn't what he professes to be, then he is trying to perpetrate a fraud upon this court."

With that, Turilli and Dill returned to Meramec Caverns, and J. Frank Dalton remained an intriguing and grumpy old man. Dalton stole his last breath on August 16, 1951, during a visit to Granbury, Texas. If he was Jesse James, he was 103 years, 11 months and 10 days old.

On July 17, 1995, George Washington University Professor of Forensics James E. Starrs exhumed the body of Jesse James buried at the grave site in Kearney, Missouri. He found the remains—discovered face-down—had sustained one bullet hole to the back of the head. He also uncovered a .36 caliber bullet among the fragments of the right ribs. Starrs found this bullet and the damage it had done in accordance with Jesse James' on-record injuries.

Known relatives of Jesse James posed for photographs with Clay County commissioners before sending the dearly departed's hair off for DNA analysis. The tests concluded with a 99.7% certainty that the body buried in Kearney was that of Jesse James. J. Frank Dalton supporters scoffed at the findings and began procedures to have their own corpse uncovered and stabbed by modern science.

Undoubtedly, Jesse James' mortal shell game will continue until all participating cadavers are propped up on crutches in a square at high noon, armed heavily and left to blast each other to mini, moldy bits. This posthumous bit of liveliness will require the services of a witch doctor, a pack of voodoo priests and the entrails of a dozen reluctant chickens, but it will make for one hell of a show.

Onondaga Cave, Missouri Caverns & Daniel Boone Park

Since the day Mark Twain popped a pail into Tom Sawyer's hand, pointed him toward Hannibal and bid him whitewash well, the fence has been an icon gently associated with Missouri. But the fence that split Onondaga Cave might have been better maintained by Hatfields and McCoys.

"Onondaga was at the time run by Bob Bradford," explains Onondaga Cave Manager, Richard Risor. "Two brothers, Dr. William and Lee Mook, leased property nearby and discovered part of the cave ran under their land. The Mooks secretly dug into the back of Onondaga. They decided their land extended to the halfway point in the Big Room, and they put up a barbed wire fence. That started an argument that almost became a shooting war the day Bob Bradford headed after Lee Mook with a rifle."

The cave that pulled itself to pieces in the early 1930s was for years seen as a simple water-filled hole. In 1881, the spring that sprung from its mouth was harnessed to power the William Davis Grist Mill. No one thought to enter the cave's soggy innards until 1886—when a drought lowered water levels and mill workers Charley Christopher, John Eaton and Mitus Horine squeezed inside in a john-boat. The trio inched their way to the cave's onyx center and left popeyed by what they had seen.

Christopher and Eaton purchased the cave. Once they owned it, they couldn't decide what to do with it. The onyx market was at its apex, but neither man had money to mine the cave. The two finally opened their cave as a tourist attraction. They called it Mammoth Cave of Missouri.

Opposite: After acquiring Onondaga in the 1950s, Lester Dill released a series of postcards featuring subterranean sweethearts.

Period photographs show Christopher, at least, made a game cave operator. Posing at stalagmites called the Twins, his manner—and moustache—betray a showman's sense. But tourists at Mammoth Cave proved almost as elusive as mining monies. In May of 1902, Eaton sold his holdings to Eugene Hunt Benoist of the Indian Creek Land Company. Christopher gave up the show cave ghost shortly afterward, selling his half of the cave to a St. Louis mining concern headed by George Bothe, Sr.

Bothe had the big bucks and equipment to mine the cave, but while he was completing core tests, the onyx market collapsed. "Builders used Missouri onyx as a substitute for marble," say Richard Risor. "But they soon realized the onyx became soft once you took it out of its natural environment." Bothe's books went soft, too, saddled with what appeared to be a pretty—but worthless—hole in the ground.

Onondaga Cave came into its own in 1904. That year, the World's Fair settled into St. Louis. Bothe did what he could to snag sightseers. A Name-the-Cave Contest earned for Onondaga its mouthful of a moniker—Iroquois for "Spirit of the Mountain"—and the Frisco Railroad brought visitors 80 miles from St. Louis to Leasburg for an inside peek. Train fare cost $1.60, and 75 cents bought a round-trip buggy ride from Leasburg to the cave. One dollar bought a ticket inside. An additional 25 cents rented a suit of state-of-the-art cave clothes.

Visitors gearing up for a 1904 trip into Onondaga found themselves loaded into flat-bottom boats and floated into the cave. The boat ride ended after a short distance, and spelunkers took to their feet for a five-hour tour. Afterward, exhausted bodies crawled into the Davis Grist Mill—newly partitioned into sleeping rooms. Daybreak found the surrey

Mammoth Cave of Missouri—Onondaga's first incarnation—was owned and operated by Charley Christopher and John Eaton. In this publicity still, the Christopher family poses. Eaton is the photographer.

waiting to trot guests back to Leasburg and the Frisco waiting there to return them to St. Louis.

After the World's Fair, Onondaga's popularity continued to grow. In 1910, Bothe sold the cave to his niece, Catherine Weinborg. She passed it along to Bob Bradford in 1913. Bradford saw a proper road reach Onondaga, but he also saw the unwelcome arrival of Dr. William and Lee Mook.

In the early 1930s, Dr. William and Lee Mook took possession of the old Benoist property. They came with plans to build a doctor's resort, but they quickly learned that Onondaga Cave ran under their land. Under cover of darkness, they entered the cave through a remote sinkhole. On a day not long afterward, an Onondaga tour guide followed an air shift inside the cave to find the Mooks improving what they claimed was their hole in the ground. The Mooks erected a barbed wire fence in the middle of Onondaga's Big Room. They named their half of the

cave Missouri Caverns and opened for tours of their own in 1932.

"Over the years, I've found spots where that fence was set up," says Onondaga Cave Manager, Richard Risor. "There's not much in the Missouri Caverns section, but the Mooks did have the Great Travertine Dome Room. The room has a natural stage and a huge dome of flowstone. At one time, Masons held meetings in it. If you go back there today, you find the entrance steps laid by the Mooks and stone tables the Masons made."

The entrance to Missouri Caverns sat closer to Route 66 than did the entrance to Onondaga Cave. The Mooks used the advantage to steal Bradford's business. Erecting a sign that read "Cave—Drive-in," they shunted sightseers into their parking lot. On occasion, sources say, they paid actors to fake automobile breakdowns in front of Missouri Caverns—to insure no car passed to reach Onondaga Cave.

Bob Bradford met these challenges with a showman's acumen—and an understandable amount of outrage. Once, Bradford threatened Lee Mook with a gun. On calmer days, Bradford won customers with his new Submarine Room. The attraction sat behind Onondaga's Lily Pad Room in a nook naturally filled with water. Bradford built a gangplank into the area and drained much of its water away to exhibit crystals formed below the waterline. He was obliged to re-drain the Submarine Room every five weeks to maintain its postcard view.

Encounters at the barbed wire fence grew common and absurd. In 1934, Missouri senatorial candidate Harry S. Truman toured Missouri Caverns with an entourage of Democrats. On the same day, a group of Republicans toured Onondaga Cave. The parties met at the barbed wire fence and spent the afternoon slinging partisan mud.

On May 7, 1935, the Supreme Court ruled on the Onondaga/Missouri Caverns dispute: The Mooks—and the fence—could stay. The news was made marginally more palatable to Bob Bradford as Dr. William Mook had died the previous November.

Missouri Caverns and Onondaga Cave operated side-by-side into the 1940s. Progressively, Onondaga Cave emerged as the dominant showplace. In 1938, Bradford dug a walk-out exit from Onondaga Cave. In 1937, Bradford built the Cool Room, a motel that sat on the banks of the Lost River immediately outside Onondaga's mouth. Bedrooms and recreational areas throughout the Cool Room's interior were chilled with genuine Onondaga Cave air.

World War II closed Missouri Caverns. By July of 1945, both Lee Mook and Bob Bradford were dead. Bradford's widow sold Onondaga Cave to Barnard Hospital.

Touring the Lost River: Bob Bradford lets Fred Bryan guide him gently down the stream.

Charles Rice, the hospital's director, had already inherited Missouri Caverns from the Mooks. He set down his stethoscope one day and realized he controlled both halves of one very troubled cave.

Rice spent the next few years piecing Onondaga back together. He tore down the barbed wire fence and rejoined Onondaga's halves. Rice demolished the Davis Grist Mill and brought electric lights into the cave. He laid new cave trails and a natural bridge that opened across King's Canopy in March of 1946. Improvements were still under way when Rice died in 1949. Four years later, Lester Dill and Lyman Riley bought Onondaga from the Rice estate.

By February of 1953, Dill and Riley were known as the King Cavemen of Franklin and Crawford Counties. Lyman was a native of Little Sioux, Iowa. A former high school teacher, he had met his wife, Velma, inside a show cave and stayed in the business. Dill was the marketing genius who brought Jesse James home to Stanton, Missouri, and painted the name of Meramec Caverns on barns across the midwest. Both men had managed Onondaga for Charles Rice. Both knew Onondaga offered things unique among Missouri show caves.

"When Mr. Dill acquired Onondaga, they still brought people into the cave by boat," says longtime Dill employee Jim Gauer. "But there was a young kid who fell out of the boat one day and drowned, and that stopped the boat trips right there."

"Apparently," explains Onondaga Cave Manager Richard Risor, "the guide stood on the front of the boat and pulled the boat along just like they usually did, and the boat capsized. That particular passage has reasonably deep water—12 to 15 feet—and the water runs underneath the rock. When the child tried to surface, she came up under that lip and drowned."

Dill fashioned a dry entrance to Onondaga. The aborted boat trips left him without a promotional angle, and he trolled television to drum up interest. Dill found his best promoter in Daniel Boone. In his day, the pioneer had traveled the Meramec River. Dill touted Onondaga as Daniel Boone's Discovery. He renamed the grounds Daniel Boone Park, dressed guides in frontier duds and christened a Daniel Boone Room along the cave trail. Dill republished the photo of Charley Christopher and family posing at Onondaga's twin stalagmites. He claimed the photo was taken at a Daniel Boone family reunion.

During the time Onondaga Cave sat inside Daniel Boone Park, coonskin caps were the fashion.

In 1967, Lyman Riley sold his interests in Onondaga Cave to Lester Dill. That same year, the venerable cave found itself at an issue's center one last time when Congress authorized construction of a dam across the Meramec River. The dam would potentially provide flood control and area recreation. Subsequent studies showed it would flood up to 80% of Onondaga's interior. Dill joined the opposition, and a bill to deauthorize the dam was introduced.

"We knew the water would fill Onondaga so far," Jim Gauer admits today. "If the dam did go in, we were ready to pin sidewalks onto the sides of the cave and install underwater lights."

Onondaga retains the feel of a cave sitting on a fence. After Dill's August 1980 death, Missouri made Onondaga a state park. Today, the cave wanders back from its quirky, commercial past. Many of the 2200 concrete steps installed by Charles Rice crumble alongside a newer, less-intrusive cave trail. Long-removed copper coins have left Lily Pad Room pools an eerie aquamarine, but tiny frogs stick to the sides of the Devil's Bathtub. Indiana Gray Bats huddle against walls, and a full 60 species of animals frequent the cave. If visitors spot wildlife in any show cave along Route 66, odds are that cave will be Onondaga. In this regard, the Spirit of the Mountain finally seems at peace.

"When I started working here," Richard Risor says, "I was told I would eventually see these people who liked to carry crystals. They'd brought a baby in one time wrapped in a deer hide, laid him down in the cave and started humming. Well, a couple of years down the road, I had a tour. They interrupted me at the Twins and said, 'We are not here for a regular tour.' I said, 'What do you want to do?' And they told me, 'We want to do our little humming thing.' That's what they did. Two or three of them actually snuck off into the darkness. I picked them up on my way back out of the cave sitting on the side of the trail with their legs folded, humming. I got a crystal out of it. It's sitting on my desk."

Above: Masons built this table which now stands secluded inside the Great Travertine Dome Room.

Right: A bat hangs from the ceiling in an old Missouri Caverns section of Onondaga Cave.

Above: Mule Trading Post mules were, from left, Susie, Sugar and Sarah. Their business partners, also from left, were Craig Culp, Scott Edwards, Karen Baden, Kurt Baden and Kurt Hilsabeck.

Right: His Hoofed Highness—the ubiquitous, gangly and completely irresistible trademark of the Mule Trading Post.

Mule Trading Post

Buzzing and blinking in overworked neon—or swabbed in searchlights under an underlit moon—trademark mascots have colored Route 66 a bold crayon bright. Consider red-feathered Pegasus heaving her hind end over the Mobil Oil marquee, or Sinclair's green dinosaur dancing gassy on the unleaded horizon. Agents of Mother Road advertising have run the gamut from fanciful to fossilized, queer, corny and sleek. On Route 66, Big Boy was born and swaddled in checkerboard overalls, Howard Johnson's Simple Simon, Pie-Man and Pooch evoked a simpler time when life was but a nursery rhyme, and the silhouette of the Jack Rabbit Trading Post loped lickety-split into sunset after commercial sunset.

Among such icons can be found one of the most whimsical—and stubborn—eye catchers the old road ever saw. Today, the long-eared, long-faced trademark of Missouri's Mule Trading Post may not strike a universally familiar chord. But once upon a time, it popped up as persistently as Porky Pig hailing the end of another Looney Tunes cartoon.

"Mules have always been associated with Missouri," says former Mule Trading Post owner, Herb Baden. "Ever since World War I when Missouri furnished most of the mules for the army. I think that's why Frank Ebling chose the name."

Like its obstinate namesake, the Mule Trading Post remains a study in persistence, a Route 66 animal that has survived 50 years through strong values and a swift, stubborn kick.

A vintage Mule Trading Post postcard puts its floppy face forward.

Founded in 1946 on the three-lane alignment of Route 66 in Pacific, Missouri, the Mule was the foal of Frank Ebling. Ebling started the Mule as a combination restaurant and gift shop, but put away the feedbag when he saw the money trinkets made. By 1955, the Mule was among the largest sellers of souvenirs in the Ozarks. When a new interstate highway blew past Route 66 between Pacific and St. Louis, Frank Ebling barely blinked. He built a new building east of Rolla and took the Mule for a slow walk southwest. The year was 1957. The Mule would not move again.

"Ashtrays were big back in the 1950s and 1960s because everybody smoked," says Herb Baden. "Plates of all sizes were popular, and cups and saucers with place names painted on them. In those days, there was a company in Chicago that pressed wood pulp to look like wood. Their stock items were religious plaques—Last Supper plaques and things like that. The company I worked for sold so many of those that during January and February—the only two months we salesmen weren't on the road—their trucks kept running to Chicago bringing full loads of this pressed wood back to Branson."

Herb Baden was an Ozark souvenir wholesaler—an ex-Exxon man with an itch in his shoes—who entered the traveling trinket market in 1955. To Baden's own surprise he was a knickknack natural. Over the seven years he worked for Lugene's Wholesale Souvenir Company of Branson, Missouri, Baden logged thousands of miles slinging ashtrays into Arkansas and souvenir pencils into Oklahoma. "Highway 66 and Lake of the Ozarks were the two biggest markets in those days," Baden explains. "That's where the big contracts were written." In Herb Baden's book, the accounts were the biggest and included Meramec Caverns, Onondaga Cave—and the Mule Trading Post.

Months on the road took Baden from his family. "One weekend I came home, and I realized my children didn't know me," he remembers. "So I realized it was time to change jobs." At the time, Interstate 70 was under construction in Illinois. Baden took a job off the new highway running a Stuckey's Pecan Shop in Altamont. He ran that Stuckey's for its first four years and found he wanted to be his own boss.

"When the Mule Trading Post came up for sale, I knew that was what I wanted," Baden admits. "I knew how good Ebling's business was from the souvenirs he used to buy from me."

Baden bought the Mule from a retiring Frank Ebling in 1966. He quickly learned the bric-a-brac business looked different from the retailer's side of the sale. One of Baden's first lessons occurred in the area of highway advertising. Unlike the majority of Route 66 tourist establishments, the Mule Trading Post had best luck when it positioned its billboards to catch travelers motoring *east*. "We learned people didn't buy souvenirs until they were returning home," says Baden. "For us, that meant people returning to the heavily populated areas of Ohio, Indiana, Illinois and Michigan." Baden also realized the Mule trademark created by Ebling was more than a homely face. Tourists loved the cartoon jackass and actively looked for him on the road. They often reported seeing him in the strangest places.

"The Mule Head logo was on every blue and yellow sign the Mule Trading Post ever had," Baden begins. "There was once over forty of them, and the only thing that differed from sign to sign was the message on the apron.

"Our signs stretched west to Joplin. All our signs were in Missouri, but people swore they saw the Mule in Texas and Oklahoma. Some people even saw the Mule in California. This happened so often, we finally decided to go along with it. Someone would tell us about some place they'd seen the Mule—some place he couldn't possibly have been. We'd say, 'Yeah. That's one sign we forgot about.'"

Backward as it seemed, the Mule's charmed life extended to changes in highway access. When Interstate 44 bypassed the Mule and devastated neighboring businesses, the Mule experienced an increase in sales. In the 1970s, when the supply of Ozark hand-woven baskets went dry, Baden found his buyers already aimed at cheaper merchandise. "Our knickknack stuff sold best—anything that said 'Missouri' or 'Ozarks' on it," Baden says. "Our back scratchers were always big sellers. They were just big pieces of bamboo cut in long strips and curved at the ends. They were cheap. They were novel. So people thought, 'This is a neat thing to buy.'"

Over the years, the Mule attracted its share of strange visitors. Barry Goldwater stopped by after his presidential hopes hit the highway. Jack Klugman sauntered in upon a slow afternoon, signed autographs and bought an odd couple of fireworks. On one occasion, an escaped mental patient appeared at the counter and announced without prejudice his intention to commit suicide on premises. Baden phoned the highway patrol and stopped the hari-kari, but not before his mother had hitched up her Bible boots. "When she heard about this fellow's intentions, she took after him with a Bible," Baden laughs. "She figured, if he was going to kill himself, at least she would convert him first."

By far the Mule's quirkiest contribution to highway lore was its Piano-Playing Chicken. The feathery Beethoven tickled ivories in the earlier 1960s. "The chicken was here and gone before I came," Baden admits. "But I had my own chicken at my Stuckeys in Altamont. The chickens were placed by this fellow from Lake of the Ozarks named Al Lechner. I knew Al from my years as a souvenir salesman. He developed these coin-operated machines with a live chicken and a little toy grand piano inside. You put in a quarter, and this chicken got the signal to peck on the piano. The minute it finished, a mechanism discharged some feed. People loved it, but one hot summer, the Humane Society put an end to it. I had to agree with them that it was cruel and inhumane. As sick as that chicken got, it would still go through its act."

In the early 1970s, Baden's teenage son and daughter approached their pop for pocket money. Baden concocted for them a pursuit that earned summer income and brought the Mule Trading Post its greatest fame. He scoured the Ozarks for a pair of gentle mules, brought them home and suggested to his children that they charge the traveling public for mule rides.

"In the summer, my daughter, my son and some of their friends sold those rides next to the store for 50 cents a ride," Baden says. "I made them give me a nickel from every ride they sold so they'd learn business is never pure profit. Pretty soon, families on vacation were lining up wanting their mule ride. My son socked away enough money leading mules

around to put himself through flying school. Today, he's a career Marine Corps pilot."

Baden chuckles when he remembers the wonder and aghast with which city slickers met his long-eared steeds. "For some, it was like admiring a zoo animal," he says. "Parents with kids love it, and old-timers would pipe up with their stories. 'I remember, when I was growing up, my grand-dad used to plow with a mule.' You'd hear those stories over and over."

When Baden's children entered college, the mule rides ended. But the Mule Trading Post trotted gamely along. Baden himself remained at its reins until March of 1995. Then—after nearly 30 years at the trading post—Baden sold the Mule to Jack and Janiece Wittmann.

Today, the Mule Trading Post survives as it always has survived—with a stubborn streak that suggests it will never go away. Back scratchers can still be bought by the itchy. And signs of Baden and his bygone burros are everywhere. Above the Trading Post's main entrance, a neon rendition of the Mule's trademark waggles its ears from half to full mast. The sign was Baden's idea. Then there's the mule barn itself. The ruddy stable raised by Baden still stands to the rear of the trading post. Across the barn's red planks, a portrait of the Mule remains. The painting was a gift to Baden from his regular sign painter. As a joke, the artist signed the portrait "Herb" for Herb Baden.

"The magic of the Mule began with its name," Baden believes. "And, of course, we always kept our restrooms clean. We visited a lot, and our prices were right. We had the Mule trademark. When Jack Wittmann bought me out, I told him, 'Whatever you do, hang onto the Mule. He's what people are going to look for. He's how they'll recognize your store.'"

In the muddy light on the edge of another Ozark day, the Mule's neon sign waggles pink neon ears. Here, slow and stubborn continues to win the race. No matter who runs this store, these walls will remain the domain of the Mule himself. A long-eared, long-faced marketing genius perhaps named Baden, perhaps named Ebling or Wittmann. Winking familiar in the public imagination, popping up on phantom signs and never—under any circumstance—saying, "That's All Folks."

Tim Jones inside his Totem Pole Trading Post—where craft and quality quietly survive.

Totem Pole Trading Post & Basketville

mong popular pastimes, basket weaving bears the brunt of more jokes than underwater ping-pong.

The activity, in fact, has been unfairly associated with the acute and chronically bonkers—a skill to be practiced in the comfortably fat corner of a padded cell. True basket weavers, think our weekend Sigmund Freuds, need knit and pearl their grassy best with one hand: They require a free index finger to go "buh-buh-buh" on their prominent bottom lips.

But along that strand of Route 66 that threads its way between Rolla and Lebanon, Missouri, an entire town once put its eggs in the basket business. In those days, Ozark meant artistry. And, as Jack D. Rittenhouse found while writing his 1946 *Guide Book to Highway 66*, the craftsmen of south-central Missouri spelled quality with a capital C:

CLEMENTINE. Hardly a town, but chiefly devoted to small roadside stands selling handmade hickory baskets and turned wood objects made by native craftsmen. The stands here are among the best of their type in the Ozarks.

"It wasn't hickory; it was white oak," Tim Jones corrects with his nose wedged in the Rittenhouse book. "Those people in Clementine could look at a tree, and they could tell you if that tree would make good baskets. They used the trunk portion. They'd split the trunk, and saw it into boards. They had a certain tool—a knife—and they'd strip the boards by hand. And then they would weave their baskets."

Eagle ears may detect some of Clementine's artistry in Tim Jones' speech. At times, Tim's words whittle subjects wistfully down to size, curling over

his shoes in a calm Missouri twang. Once inspired, his hands tie the air in enough knots to knit a hay howdah for an elephant. Tim talks of Clementine, and he talks of the Old Wire Road. Tallest among his subjects stands his own Totem Pole Trading Post.

Harry Cochran built the first Totem Pole in 1933—several miles west of the current store—and atop a rise called Arlington Hill. An Indiana native, Cochran built his establishment of logs. At its start, the Totem Pole offered a gift shop, a restaurant, a Standard Oil station and six log tourist cabins. Cochran later added a coin-operated laundromat— the first coin-operated laundromat in Phelps County. Over all, Cochran erected an enormous totem pole. The skillfully carved noodle—a wooden stream of fish, snakes and grumpy devils—stood on the roof of the original Totem Pole for almost 30 years— relinquishing its place in 1961 when the gift shop and restaurant were remodeled into one building.

Talk of coming highway woes convinced Cochran to sell. He listed the Totem Pole with an agent in St. Louis and caught the interest of Ralph Jones. Jones was a former Californian who had spent a good portion of his youth on the trick-riding circuit, trotting along in a troupe headed by western film actor, Victor McClonklin. He'd spent his last six years working for IBM and yearned to be self-employed. He bought the Totem Pole in 1957.

"Harry Cochran was living in the past," Ralph Jones says of the man who sold him his livelihood. "He wasn't stocking the place. He thought Catherine and I wouldn't make it. The highway was going to change, and they were talking about closing Fort Leonard Wood. But we filled the place up and stayed open seven days a week from six in the morning to eleven at night. The buyers were there."

Tiskets, taskets and baskets: The original Totem Pole built by Harry Cochran.

Ralph Jones kept the Totem Pole's six cabins closed to tourist traffic. The cabins had been listed in Jack Rittenhouse's 1946 *Guide Book to Highway 66*, but Jones saw them as warehouses that permitted him to buy merchandise in bulk. Each cabin came to keep one kind of item—one stored fireworks; another held pottery; a third kept chairs and stools. One nearly burst with baskets from Basketville.

At the time the Jones family took control of the Totem Pole, nearby Clementine—or Basketville—had passed its crafty prime. Construction of dual roadways in the early 1950s had reduced by half the number of cars passing in front of its businesses. But descendants of the first basket weavers still wove their skillful best.

Henry Jasper Childers had more to do with the rise of handicraft at Clementine than anyone else. Childers came to Clementine in 1928 from Cabool,

Missouri, looking for a place to profit from his extensive woodworking skills. He squeezed his family into a modest log cabin and opened a woodworking shop next-door.

Childers' sign advertised *Artful Woodwork Made by Ozark Hillbillies*. He sold baskets and baby cradles, footstools and chairs. Tourists couldn't get enough of his carefully-crafted stock. Childers' shop became the area's biggest business.

Other Clementine artisans took up the basket trade. Darius "Dan" Bartram opened the Ozark Gift Shop. In 1938, Carl Becker arrived from New York to start a wholesale business in ladder-back, straight-back and rocking chairs made of cherry, walnut, oak and ash. The basket business spilled west into Pulaski County and Hooker, Missouri, where Ruth and Clarence Wells kept a shop. The Wells supplied baskets to the Totem Pole Trading Post.

Woven wares throughout Clementine were commonly displayed on wires strung near the highway's edge. The Totem Pole adopted this practice—setting its artistic inventory outside each morning and bringing it back inside each eve. Everyday setup could take more than an hour. Ralph Jones often assigned the task to his young son, Tim.

"I started working at the Totem Pole when I was ten," Tim Jones says. "The first Totem Pole was built on a curve. When it began to rain, cars would come around that curve and slide into our driveway. We had our gas pumps knocked out repeatedly.

"One time, me and a friend were tending the gas station. It started to sprinkle rain, and here comes this Volkswagen. The lady driving—she'd cut the wheel too fast—and this car was actually bouncing down the road. It landed on its wheels, and we ran to see if anyone was hurt. When we looked inside, all we could see were two pairs of legs sticking up over the seat. Then we heard one lady say to the other, 'Mabel, honey, are you all right? Last time, you went through the windshield.'"

In 1961, the Totem Pole closed its restaurant and opened a saddle shop. Harry Cochran's carved totem pole came off the roof, and a large painted cowboy was constructed to stand near the road. The colossal wrangler wore a pair of blue jeans several stories high. "They were real jeans," Ralph Jones says. "As a promotion, a blue jean company gave us a pair of jeans about 25-feet long. We put 'em on the cowboy to advertise our western wear." Tourists stopped in herds to snap photos of the big buckaroo.

In 1966, Interstate 44 construction began. The state came to claim the Totem Pole's buildings. Outraged by the meager offer the state made for his property, Ralph Jones rallied local merchants to a legal battle that lasted ten years. In the end, the merchants were permitted to pick an appraiser. Area property owners were reasonably compensated.

The Totem Pole rebuilt itself three miles west of Rolla—in a building that today houses Gauntlet Paint. A rough decade later, the state prepared to make that stretch of road limited access. The highway negotiators returned. "When that happened, my dad threw his hands in the air," says Tim Jones. "He didn't have any fight left." Tim Jones and his brother Bill bought the Totem Pole from their father in 1974. Tim bought out Bill in 1976.

As the Interstate isolated area businesses, Clementine died a lonely commercial death. The basket stores at Hooker persisted into the 1970s, then they, too, gave up the artful ghost.

Left: With Ralph Jones in the background, Michael and Bill Jones smile and say, "Souvenirs." Right: Jones children trot past the pottery shed on their pet pony.

In 1978, the Totem Pole moved to its present location on Rolla's western rim and into a two-bay Shell gas station that has since expanded in every direction. Here, among buffalo-bone toothpicks, mosquito traps and other novelty items, one finds Tim Jones and his wife Alice today. The carved totem pole that stood atop the original store now stands near the cash register. An upstairs addition is graced, at either end, by stained glass windows from a Rolla church. The addition was completed shortly before the Jones' 20-year-old son was killed in a car accident. The young man's portrait rests in tribute against a Totem Pole column and reminds travelers the road can bring heartbreak as easily as happiness.

"Times have changed since the baskets went out and came in every day," Tim says at the end of an afternoon visit. "I didn't realize how good things were back then. The harder you worked—the more was out there. Ruth and Clarence Wells made baskets for us for 40 years. They made 39 styles of baskets—all of white oak. They taught me how to do it. And I learned how difficult—how very slow and time consuming—that process was. In this day and age, artists like that would be very hard-pressed to make a living."

Down the road, in a quiet place called Clementine, no comment is forthcoming. The weavers have shuttered their shops, and the dance of their fingers is a thing no longer seen. When Route 66 surrendered Clementine, it lost more than a souvenir community. It lost something that survives only in pockets like the Totem Pole Trading Post. Something that can only be called QUALITY— spelled with capitals—in a very human hand.

A PLACE CALLED BASKETVILLE

Left: Henry J. Childers, the father of Clementine handicraft, stands with some of his fancier baskets. The large basket sold for $5. The smaller baskets sold for 25 cents each.

Right: Clarence Wells creates white oak strips.

Center: The Childers workshop virtually worked like an artful assembly line. Left to right, Harry Thompson, George Ruckman, Andrew Childers, Chester Ruckman, William F. Childers, George Ruckman, Jr.

Left: Woven wares displayed prominently to attract the motoring eye.

Santa Claus greets visitors inside Onyx Mountain Caverns' Dripstone Room.

King Cave, Onyx Cave Park & Onyx Mountain Caverns

Tradition tells a tale of Santa living at the North Pole, tinkering with toys and shooing walrus from his sidewalk. But the stone show inside Onyx Mountain Caverns leaves old Kringle between a rock and a hard place.

"Santa Claus was discovered by Hell's Angels," tour guide Craig Thiltgen says of the caverns' most festive formation. "I had a tour of about 20 of them come through five years ago. One guy kept pointing and saying 'Santa Claus!' I kept asking him what he saw, because Santa Claus was the last name I expected to hear. Turned out these Hell's Angels were from Chicago, and they were riding to Springfield, Missouri, for Toys for Tots."

The fossilized face of Father Christmas heads up the flights of fancy in Onyx Mountain Caverns' Dripstone Room—a haven for onyx icicles that crowns the caverns' current tour. Natural forces have slapped Santa's face a jolly, jelly-red and placed at his cheek a puny, green pixie. The colors seem contrived—too perfect to be true—until one understands the low-lying Onyx Mountain Caverns have for years schooled students in geological firsts and only recently received widespread credit.

Like a granite cat with umpteen lives, the caverns that lie 11 miles west of Rolla have harbored a number of histories under a lapful of different names. Originally called King Cave for its huge entrance room, the cave was re-christened Onyx Cave after Victorian miners had their way with the white stone inside. In recent years, the name Onyx Mountain Caverns graces this grotto that saw its first lantern-luggers before the nineteen-teens.

"For many years, the Frisco Railroad ended passenger service at Jerome," says Onyx Mountain Caverns owner, Harry Thiltgen. "Jerome was at that time a resort town filled with hotels and cabins. Excursion boats were at the service of anybody who wanted to come to this cave. The boats would bring 'em up river, and they'd be met at the river by riding horses. They'd ride the quarter mile from the river up to the cave, and a guide would show 'em the entrance room by kerosene lamp. That was your basic cave tour in 1909.

"During WPA years, *A Guide to the 'Show Me' State* was published. The guide outlined different drives you could take in Missouri. The drive for this area started at Stony Dell Resort and came up an unmarked gravel road here to Onyx Cave Park. Onyx Cave Park was a whole complex of buildings. There was a dance hall, restaurants, cabins, horse shoe pits —the whole nine yards. Guides would walk visitors down and into the cave entrance for 35¢ a head."

Harry Thiltgen has owned Onyx Mountain Caverns for ten years. He's lived in the Phelps County area for the last 35. In the spring of 1964, he began a 14-year stint operating nearby Boiling Springs Resort on the Gasconade River, quitting only when advancing age made rising to bait early-morning bass fishermen a bother. In the later 1980s, Harry bought the property on which Onyx Cave and old Onyx Cave Park sat. He opened the cave as a formal attraction in August of 1990.

"The day before we officially opened," says Harry, "I was contacted by an elderly lady who had been a school superintendent in Newburg. She said, 'I got my niece and her husband here from California, and they have to leave tomorrow. Is there any way we can see the cave today?' I told her, 'Sure.' She brought them down, and her son-in-law turned out to be John Sheffield—the kid who played the Son of Tarzan in the old movie series. Well, he didn't swing from stalactites when he was in the cave, but I still think it's interesting the first person to take the modern tour was a celebrity."

Since time immemorial, the large Entrance Room has been the cave's biggest draw. Behind an entrance hole that measures 420 by 100 feet, a village of Woodland Indians once lived—cooking, communing and bickering with each other. Today, the 10,000-year-old ash they left behind covers the floor to a depth of 25 feet.

The ash continues to burp up artifacts. Among the bear bones, turtle shells and mussel shells, strange pancake-shaped stones routinely emerge. "More than likely, the stones were brought up from the river," ventures tour guide Craig Thiltgen, "but we don't know exactly what they were used for. The Indians could have heated them over the fire and used them to cook. They could have used them for games. Or they could have thrown them at kids when they got mad."

To a greater degree than other show caves along Missouri Route 66, Onyx Mountain Caverns fills spelunkers' plates with simple education. Interpretive placards pepper its cave trail. Makeshift beds stuffed with deer moss illustrate a Woodland Indian's idea of a posture-pedic mattress.

A blueprint stands self-importantly at a turn in the trail. The working drawing is all that remains of a scrapped 1951 Navy plan to buy the cave and build a Hydro-Cavern inside—a type of jet-propulsion laboratory to test engines for fighter planes. Progress in missile systems aborted the mission.

The temperature inside Onyx Mountain Caverns remains a cool 55 degrees—a few points cooler than the average Missouri show cave. Over one wall, an eerie gray matter splatters like yesterday's salad. The flaky mess is actually an ancient species of algae— one that exists nowhere else in the world. "It's also tropical," puts in Craig. "No one can figure out why it's growing here at this temperature. They think it started growing when the whole world was a tropical

Photograph taken inside Onyx Mountain Caverns—then called Onyx Cave—in the 1940s.

In its day, Stony Dell saw many of its guests sneaking off to explore nearby Onyx Cave. The popular resort, built by George Prewett, was located one mile west of Arlington on Route 66.

rain forest and gradually adapted as temperatures changed. They discovered it in 1991. They're running tests on it down at the University of Florida. They want to find out if it cures any disease."

Past Onyx Mountain Caverns' underground stream—and beyond the turn-off for the unctuous passage affectionately known as Peanut Butter Alley—enlightenment takes a one-of-a-kind turn. In an area pimpled with pits the Woodland Indians used as portable refrigerators, the tour halts to boldly point out scars made by modern man. Onyx Mountain Caverns—alone among the show caves off Missouri 66—was commercially mined. In 1892, a shaft was sunk into its belly and great chunks of its personality were carted away courtesy of the

Imperial Onyx Mining Company. To the credit of Onyx Mountain Caverns, the sightseer is steered headlong into the cracked and broken carnage left by miners' tools—to a place where bolts and drill holes crucify the ceiling and the only solid stalactites are imperfect and marbled. The view is disturbing and caps off the day's classroom activities with one of the hardest lessons nostalgia buffs can learn: Sometimes, progress helps. Sometimes, modern sensibilities save treasures by the seats of their pants.

"Of course, these days, Santa Claus is having an affair with Marge Simpson," Craig Thiltgen adds as he focuses his flashlight on another Dripstone Room formation.

You learn something new every day.

Above: An invitation to sleep in Storybook Land—Nelson Dream Village.
Below: The central attraction of Nelson Dream Village—Colonel Nelson's Musical Fountain.

The Musical Fountain at Nelson Dream Village

ust for kicks on one Mesopotamian afternoon—and with intent to tickle his Median wife—the 6th century B.C. Babylonian ruler Nebuchadnezzar II unpacked his potting soil, stacked stone tiers tastefully to the moon and strung up the Hanging Gardens of Babylon.

Colonel Arthur T. Nelson of Lebanon, Missouri, could have told old Nebbie how to achieve the effect with a string of snapdragons and a tinkling cherub.

After all, the man who broke landscaping ground along Route 66 commanded a bumper crop of Lebanon's lushest land. His apple orchard bordered the Ozark playground, an area rocked heavier than any casbah and splashed greener than St. Patrick on a jealous afternoon. In his earlier days, the colonel won a gold medal for 75 barrels of apples exhibited at the Paris Exposition. On standing order, he supplied fruit to England's royal family.

Arthur's life took its agricultural turn in 1882 when he moved with his parents from New York to Lebanon, Missouri. Arthur's father established an enormous apple orchard in Laclede County. Arthur used these family trees to climb to public promi-nence. In all, nine consecutive Missouri governors found Arthur the apple of their political eyes. They appointed him to posts on the State Fair Board and the Marketing, Penal and Highway Commissions. One governor suited Arthur with the honorary title of colonel. Arthur popped the title into his personality and wore it like a rose.

From his earliest years, Colonel Arthur T. Nelson remained fascinated with road travel. As early as 1913, he used a truck to haul produce to market. A 1915 family trip left him championing the brick streets of Indiana.

Once in position to plant seeds in powerful ears, the colonel began lobbying for fine Missouri roads. The state suggested Route 14 cut through his land. The colonel allocated a 40-acre tract for this road that would become Route 66. Then he noticed—as he was patting himself on his broad civic back—that the road crews were killing his fruit trees.

Colonel Nelson was a member of the State Board of Agriculture. He was a lifetime member of the State Horticulture Society. He well knew when to pull up roots. When his son, Frank, suggested he build a service station and try his hand at a highway trade, the colonel turned in his apples for oil cans. On July 3, 1926, he opened the Nelson Service Station and Rest Rooms on Route 66.

Surprise awaited anyone who believed the colonel had hung up his garden hose. In a day before gas stations became boxes with bubble signs—and "highway beautification" was a strange and unusual term—the colonel had constructed a roadside work of art. His service station was not as much a grease pit as it was a rock garden with pumps. Quaint cobblestones formed its walls. Pristine pillars marked driveways. A flower bed 5 feet wide by 460 feet long offered oodles of rose for the nose.

A hamburger stand served anyone who grew peckish smelling posies. The counter had plenty of customers as more and more travelers thought the colonel's station a good place to park for the night.

"There were hotels on the railroad, but that was three blocks from the highway," explains the colonel's granddaughter, Beth Nelson Owen. "People wanted to stay right at the service station, so the colonel put up a bath house with six tents on either side. People rented those tents for a dollar a night. They were always full, so he built cottages."

Top O' the Ozarks Camp gave way to 12 cabins, each named for a different state. The small lunch counter grew into a short-order diner called Top O' the Ozarks Inn. By 1930, the colonel and his son, Frank, had torn down Top O' the Ozarks Inn and grafted the Nelson Tavern onto the end of the service station. The two-story study in stucco and emerald trim began business with a grand opening celebration on Tuesday, January 21, and spent the next several years ushering customers into a dining room that could have doubled as a greenhouse.

Tables and desks inside Nelson Tavern were buried under crops of vegetables. Vases burst with rare flowers. Palm trees glutted the lounge, and exotic birds peeped between these—fluttering in decorative cages. Upstairs, two communal bathrooms served 22 guest rooms filled with velvet carpets and Beauty Rest mattresses. Guest windows looked out onto the grounds. By now, it was a jungle out there: Shredded sumac, dogwood and sassafras filled the yard. A large red sunflower stared unblinking into a pond swimming with goldfish.

The colonel planted 40,000 gladiolus bulbs in and around the tavern—165 varieties of which were imported from Germany, France, Australia and New Zealand. The sea of blossoms obliged the colonel to employ a full-time gardener. The *Lebanon Rustic* called the area Nelsonville—"the best known spot on Highway 66 between Chicago and Los Angeles." Reports surfaced of families traveling an extra 100 miles in a day simply to sleep under Nelsonville's fragrant spell.

"Pretty Boy Floyd ate in the dining room," says Beth Nelson Owen. "So did the Phillip Morris bellboy. If you remember the little boy—he was a midget, I guess—who went through the theater with a plate on one hand hollering 'Call for Phillip Morris!' He came to Nelson's Tavern to eat. Mother always said he was very rude. He was the type of person impressed by his own importance. He threw around what little bit of weight he had."

In 1933, Colonel Nelson took the Missouri exhibit to Chicago's Century of Progress Exhibition. There he encountered a contraption that haunted his landscaping dreams: a musical fountain rigged to work with colorful, synchronized lights.

In 1934, the colonel literally went to bed and dreamed he saw that fountain spouting music at the center of a tourist court. He arose the next morning claiming he had seen Fairyland. He set down his dream in a sketch that became the blueprint for Nelson Dream Village.

Nelson Dream Village would be the colonel's greatest achievement. The colonel himself told the newspapers so before construction began. On the north side of Route 66—across the highway from Nelson's Tavern—the cottages sprang up in a semicircle. There would be 12 in all, each constructed of native stones the colonel had personally approved. Red and white sandstone, lava bed rock, river-washed stone and field stone were stacked into storybook walls. Rock chimneys topped off the Hansel-and-Gretel flavor.

The marquee musical fountain sat in the center of Dream Village's manicured courtyard. The colonel built the fountain himself, to a diameter of 26 feet. He dug his own well to keep the fountain filled and wired electricity to its lights.

A St. Louis company was contracted to provide maintenance for the mechanism. Other technicalities were not so easily solved. Modern-day musical fountains are computer synchronized. They often light to 125,000 watts and blare their ballads through 12,000-watt speakers. The colonel had colored bulbs in hand, but he had no digital audio system in the bush. Limitations demanded he find an easy means to take his concert to the outside air.

"The colonel played records over a loudspeaker," says Beth Nelson Owen. "My sister and I handled that. Dream Village had a central building that was the office. That's where we were—with a record player and a selection of records. We took one record off and put another record on, and that's what we did all summer. We played nothing in popular music. Just light classicals. The colonel was a real music lover. He preferred Viennese waltzes, and he made the program."

The trickling concert at Nelson's Dream Village commenced at dusk each evening with no formal announcement and tumbled through ten formations for a watery hour. Colored lights played over unsynchronized jet sprays, but few guests counted beats.

A postcard advertising the Musical Fountain. The girl at water's edge is Beth Nelson Owen.

Most audience members watched from unheated cars—a fact that dictated how far into the fall the fountain played. Many fountain fans were locals, and a good number came from neighboring towns. Although benches had been placed on either side of the fountain, spectators rarely used them. Guests overnighting at Nelson Dream Village typically sat on the settees that stood outside their cabin's door.

The colonel himself took pleasure in his tuneful attraction. As his years trickled away, he often sat and watched the fountain—nodding to the music his granddaughters played. As Beth Nelson Owen grew to adulthood, she preferred to play the *Blue Danube Waltz.* By all indications, the colonel was pleased with her maturing musical tastes.

In October of 1936, Colonel Arthur T. Nelson died. In 1944, Frank Nelson leased the Nelson Tavern—now called the Nelson Hotel—to Mr. and Mrs. C. Lynn West. West became an active citizen of Lebanon, serving as mayor, city councilman and president of the Highway 66 Association.

Lebanon became one of the first Missouri towns bypassed by the interstate. On July 29, 1958, the Nelsons sold the hotel property to the Wheeler Market Company of Springfield, Missouri. The hotel and gas station were subsequently razed.

Dream Village survived into the 1970s—long after the highway that weaned it had been demoted to a city street. Frank Nelson died. His widow, Dorothy, did her best to keep Dream Village afloat. Overnight guests turned into weekly renters, and Dorothy gave the motel to her children. They saw fit to sell the property. "My youngest son asked for the mechanism that had been in the fountain," says Beth Nelson Owen. "We told him he could have it, but before he got out there, it was stolen."

Nelson Dream Village was demolished in the summer of 1977.

Lebanon, Missouri—like many Route 66 towns—remains a place that has lost a good deal of its classic establishments. But unlike most Mother Road towns, Lebanon has retained more of its Route 66 flavor than it has lost. Much of the credit for this rests with green thumbs like Colonel Arthur T. Nelson who believed in planting community pride between azaleas and elm trees. Pause in Lebanon. Pin a posie in your lapel. And know character—above all—is what the old road naturally grew.

Shirley Lang has an argument with the lion cub in her charge at Exotic Animal Paradise.

Buena Vista's Exotic Animal Paradise

Charles Darwin started this world thinking about the banana-thin line between man and monkey. Nowhere along Route 66 can the ape-to-executive link be better appreciated than at Buena Vista's Exotic Animal Paradise.

"Put your arm around her," Director of Marketing Randy Clutter instructs the male half of a twenty-something couple standing before the baboon cage at Safari Center. The day is fine and filled with music warbling from a loud speaker. From his seat behind steel bars, Casey the baboon looks from Randy to the wide-eyed couple.

"Put your arm around her," Randy repeats.

The young man does as he's told—slinging a limb around his sweetie's shoulder. In the shortest of spans, the boxed monkey goes ape—rattling his bars like a double-crossed convict. Casey's spectacle is vicious and filled with snarls and spit, but Randy, unflustered, snickers.

"See?" Randy laughs. "Casey's jealous. He does have a ton of personality."

At Exotic Animal Paradise, four-footed encounters are of the closest kind. Billing itself as "America's Largest and Greatest Drive-Through Wild Animal Park," Exotic Animal Paradise lives up to its chest-beating with more than a wildebeest to spare. The spotted, striped and horned heads here come closer to one's nose than one usually allows smellier relatives—huffing and puffing and invading cars by the hairs of their chinny-chin-chins. The only escape involves rolling up windows, and this would be a serious sin against Nature. There's a little Dr. Dolittle in all of us—an African explorer who would love to find an elephant in his pajamas.

Contact sports, after all, sit comfortably in the park founder's family tree. Exotic Animal Paradise was forged by Springfield insurance tycoon John Watson "Pat" Jones, whose son, Jerry Jones, would become the owner of the Dallas Cowboys.

Look who's coming to dinner: The beastly eaters at Exotic Animal Paradise eat easily from anyone's outstretched hand.

Long before his son turned to pigskin, the elder Jones rounded up peacocks. A native of England, Arkansas, his rags to rhinos story began with stops in the gardenia, grocery and drive-in businesses and reached its apex only after he'd stopped to see a disappointing animal attraction in Dallas.

"At first, Pat collected animals for his own pleasure," explains Exotic Animal employee Naoma Robinson. "But more and more people wanted him to share what he had, so he started building a permanent animal farm here—close to the highway. My cousin was one of the bulldozer operators. He told me Pat would crawl on the bulldozer with him and say, 'Leave this tree, but take this one out. Here, I want you to dig me a lake.' There were no formal plans. The park was designed in Pat's head as he drove through on the heavy equipment."

Exotic Animal Paradise opened in the summer of 1971—along a section of Route 66 that was once imbued with rambling rose bushes. The beautiful blooms grew along the fence line from the top of Northview Hill into Springfield. Some say they marked an area of professional hanky-panky.

"This used to be the old Holman Ranch," says Director of Marketing, Randy Clutter. "On it, sat the Ranch Hotel. The hotel was a bit of a hunting lodge. It's our understanding that wealthy hunters would come to the Holman Ranch. And they would come hunting four-legged deer and *two-legged* deer."

For Randy, Exotic Animal Paradise represents a third profession. A retired captain of the Springfield police, he built a life in law enforcement atop an earlier career in the entertainment industry. Randy's comrade in zebu cows is Director of Operations Rick Sanders—a San Antonian and former animal wrestler who has looked after exotic animals for a full twenty years. Together they make a formidable Stanley and Livingstone—ironing out burrs and brambles from the back office both affectionately call the War Room, dealing with pregnant giraffes, range cubes and the latest gnus.

"Animals are truer to you—good or bad—than people," Rick insists. "I remember one situation I had in the hills of southern Oklahoma. It was a dark, moonless night. We had a rhino that was loose, and we had maybe eight or ten guys that were trying to find this rhino.

"I was in a big one-ton truck, and I parked in the middle of the road, got out and stood in front of the truck listening. And you know how you sometimes cup your hand to your ear, thinking you might hear better? Well, I did that. What I didn't know: There was a big, bull elk about ten feet from me, standing on the road. And he bugled. I jumped, and when I turned around, I ran face first right into that truck. Every bit of air ran out of me. While I was lying there, I could hear the elk running off, and then I realized: I'd scared him as much as he'd scared me."

Along the second and wilder half of the Exotic Animal Paradise tour, rival elk lock horns.

The safari proper at Exotic Animal Paradise is one of the few in the world accessible from the seat of a Chevy Cavalier. Beyond the ticket booths of civilization—and armed with bags of feed purchased for nominal fees—visitors enter a veritable box of animal crackers poking their noses at car windows and begging handfuls of anything edible. Gruff billy goats block bridges and demand pellets for passage. Gentle giraffes slobber over glove boxes, and llamas prove themselves masterminds at stopping vehicles in their tracks. A sign warning "Keep Windows Up Around Bears and Monkeys" heads up the second and more exotic leg of the trip. From that point forward, it's every ape for himself.

"The ostrich are a lot of fun," Randy says from the safety of the War Room. "When you get into a herd of ostrich out there, they'll steal everything you've got. They take your tools; they take your supplies; if you leave your window down, your notes are taken out of the truck."

"We do hay rides," adds Rick, "and on one occasion we had a senior citizens group. They were feeding ostrich. If you've ever seen an ostrich eat, they eat with vigor. You hold this cup for 'em, and they attack the food. Well, this man spilled his food in his lap. The ostrich really didn't care where the food was. And they went for it. That poor guy had some very anxious moments."

Along the trails of Exotic Animal Paradise there exists plenty of opportunity to compare wits with the wilder things in life. The park could be called an alfresco I. Q. test pairing human intelligence against animal instinct. Humans, most often, come up short. A few years ago, park officials decided a gaggle of geese might add to the public area ambiance and clipped a few Canadian wings. Today, honkers flock everywhere and refuse to migrate in wintry months. On rare occasions, nature-struck knuckleheads step out of cars to photograph dangerous animals. And then there's the incident that occurred some years ago during the park's holiday light show called Christmas in Paradise. The million-bulb festival is a light-lover's dream—an eye-boggling spectacle of great times and good cheer that begins the second week in November and flickers through the first of January. Merrymakers enjoy Santa's Cottage and live theatrical shows that play every twenty minutes in a renovated War Room. But Randy begs all comers: Please don't peel your candy canes under the Peacock Tree.

"The peacocks have a favorite tree where they go to roost at night," Randy begins. "It's a big tree, and it's right over the sidewalk. Well, the people were coming in droves for the lights, and they would walk under this tree and notice that those were real peacocks roosting up there. Groups of people would be standing under that tree saying, 'See the peacocks?' You tell people, 'Don't stand there! Don't stand there!' You do that every ten minutes. Finally you give up, and you stand aside and let Nature take its course. That seems to be a better lesson, because once *it* happens, that sidewalk clears out pretty fast."

Joking aside, animal schooling remains a matter of staff pride at Exotic Animal Paradise. Bouncing bundles of fluff are as a matter of routine taken home by workers until they're large enough to stand with their elders. Randy himself babied Buckwheat, one of three lion cubs whose birth, along with those of Spanky and Alfalfa, marked a particularly rascally year. The mothering bond between human and beast is perhaps best exhibited by gift shop supervisor Shirley Lang arriving to work with a lion cub on a leash. "I wanted to take home the bear cubs—those were the neat little guys," says Shirley. "When Ben—the boy cub—got cranky, I used to rock him to sleep. Just like I did with my son."

As the lunch hour looms and music trickles through the loud speakers around Safari Center, Randy Clutter walks amid the claws and catcalls of his world. Casey, the he-man baboon, presents Randy with a flaming view of his rump, but Randy continues past the lion cubs, around the dreaded Peacock Tree and up against a cage that contains a skittish and harmless looking simian. "I suppose my favorite animal is this little spider monkey," Randy admits, extending his monkey friend a noontime treat. "I enjoy feeding him once in awhile, and we just kind of got to be buddies. I enjoy coming here to see Spidey."

"Of course," Rick cracks, "he frankly realizes there's a close family tie."

And laughter chatters from the trees.

Photograph
by Harry Morgan.

Looking from back
showing Entrance

Crystal Cave

Whenever a car horn honks, Agnes, the oldest, is the first one to go.

Her aging hands take flashlights from their store place near the door; brittle fingers find buttons and snug her warm against the cold. As Agnes shuffles out the screen door, twelve dogs bark her slow departure: an adopted canine dozen of Greene County's finest strays.

The sign that hugs the tree reads: Stop. Honk Loud for Information. *Agnes never sees it as she ambles down the hill. She's tread this trail a thousand times; she might be walking in her sleep. But, underfoot, the grass is brown with recent clippings—proof her sister Margaret has diligently mowed. The grass would be quite greener on the threshold of a dream.*

At the gate that guards the entrance to the cave, Agnes stops and waits. Sightseers swing clear of their cars and eagerly come forward. Agnes pulls the portal open. Perhaps, today, Robert L. Ripley will return to look at that tree root that grows inside the cave. Perhaps, tomorrow, Harry S. Truman will bring his calling card. Whoever comes, they will find Agnes and her two sisters ready to meet them as long as they can manage: personable and polite, in prim and proper dress.

Patiently holding open the stony mouth of Time.

To a cave, time means little. Lounging on a limestone bed, sipping silt through a million soda straws, caves decline to brush bats from their hair or moss from their mouths for months, centuries, eons at a leap.

Not so with hurried Homo sapiens. On the all-too-human road, time becomes a ticking bomb Fingers drum waiting on red to change to green. Rest stops welcome marathon runners. National Parks become revolving doors made of ferns and waterfalls.

In a pocket of Greene County, Missouri, Crystal Cave soothes students of the Pedal-to-the-Metal School. This nook that naps north of Springfield has been a haven for harried traffic for over 100 years. In spite of this century's alarm clocks and egg timers, odds say it will remain so for many thousands more. No one minds a watch here. No one counts sand through an hourglass or days of our lives.

Opposite: An early photo taken inside Crystal Cave.

"We stay just about as busy as two old people should be," says current cave owner, Loyd Richardson. "We just take it real slow so people can enjoy. This is our retirement job; we don't try to make a lot of money."

Crystal Cave's restful nature hardly surprises. Its developer's first business was selling padding on which people could sleep. Alfred Mann was an Englishman born in Brighton and schooled in France. He made his first trip to America at age 17 and spent three years loping around the country before returning to England to marry and father four children. In 1882, Mann moved his family to Salina, Kansas. Five years later, he opened Springfield Mattress, Bed Spring and Upholstery Works at 1301 Boonville Street in Springfield, Missouri. The works did a comfortable business selling mattresses stuffed with hair, moss, cotton and wool, but Mann grew weary of it all the same. One day, he swapped the whole kit and caboodle for Crystal Cave—and the 140 acres under which the cave sat.

Alfred Mann's mattress shop was located on Boonville Street in Springfield, Mo. The Mann family lived in a small apartment above the store—a situation that may have inspired Mann to trade the entire business for Crystal Cave.

Mann had seen the uses to which caves were put in France. After building a farmhouse for his family, he fashioned his cave into an underground nursery. He stacked native stones into planting beds and raised mushrooms and rhubarb in the cave's large entrance room. For a time, the fruits—and fungus—of his labor sold throughout the state. But Mann's own underground intrigue got the better of him. He thought the cave beautiful, and he longed to share its sights with an appreciative public eye. In 1893, he followed the lead of Mark Twain Cave in Hannibal, Missouri, and opened Crystal Cave as the second show cave in the Show Me State.

Early-day admission at Crystal Cave was ten cents per head. Hewn steps placed by Mann led visitors through the cave's entrance room—now filled with empty planting beds—and into fanciful chambers named by Mann and his family. One formation in the Rocky Mountain Chamber enjoyed such popularity that it drew the attention of the Smithsonian Institute and earned itself a new name.

"They first called that formation the Twin Castles," Loyd Richardson says of the cave's most famous feature. "But they changed the name to the Washington Monument for the pools of standing water in front of it. When the cave first opened, it was one of the main attractions. Mr. Mann gave the Smithsonian Institute permission to make a scale model of the formation for their cave display. Today, you can still see that replica in Washington, D.C."

During Crystal Cave's early years, the Mann family reached Springfield by horse and buggy.

The trip took three hours. The isolation encouraged family interdependence, and the Mann children were assigned duties in the cave in addition to their household chores.

At a Fourth of July celebration in Springfield's Sequoyah Park, the Mann's nine-year-old son, Willie, was accidentally killed. The loss left Alfred Mann emotionally scarred. As his three daughters became adults, Mann found himself incapable of loosening his parental grip. When middle daughter, Ada, became engaged to neighbor William Funkhouser, Mann set about constructing a cottage on Crystal Cave property to keep the bride and groom close to home. He went so far as to stock the cabin with wicker furniture. The Mann sisters called the cabin Honeymoon Cottage. William Funkhouser called it impossible, broke the engagement and left for the far west as fast as his legs could carry him. Eventually, he settled in Arkansas and married Cora Southard. Ada Mann never married. Neither did the other Mann sisters.

In 1926, Alfred Mann died. Mrs. Mann died in 1930, and care of Crystal Cave fell to sisters Agnes, Ada and Margaret. The three divided cave-keeping chores between themselves—as they had shared chores as children: Agnes became principle tour guide. Ada became business manager and automobile driver, and Margaret took charge of the cooking and grounds upkeep. Ever wary of attracting more customers than they could comfortably handle, the Mann sisters hung a few signs along the highway and called their advertising complete.

The entire Mann family—including the unfortunate young Willie—pose inside Crystal Cave for this promotional still. Kerosene chandeliers swing over the scene.

The Mann sisters, from left, Ada, Margaret and Agnes. "They always wore some kind of hat," says Edith Richardson. "Most of the time when you'd see them, they'd have on men's jumpers with coats and long skirts. Even though they were giving cave tours, they wouldn't have thought about putting on a pair of blue jeans. That would have been terrible."

The Mann sisters told reporters they preferred to conduct cave tours in a leisurely fashion. True to their word, they refused to prod visitors along. On one occasion, a gentleman from Kansas City strolled through the cave while campaigning for senator. Years later, Margaret found his card among old cave papers and saw that his name was Harry S. Truman. Over another afternoon, an inquisitive chap stayed to study a living root that had wiggled its way into the cave from a mulberry tree over 70 feet above. He introduced himself as Robert L. Ripley, and he featured the root in his *Believe It or Not!* column.

In time, William Funkhouser's family moved back to his boyhood home. Ada Mann bore no animosity toward her ex-fiance's family. She and William's widow became close friends. All three Mann sisters grew particularly fond of the Funkhousers' daughter, Estle. Estle adored the three Mann sisters and cared for them as they entered their autumn years.

"Estle wasn't married, either," says Estle's sister, Edith Richardson. "That's one reason the Mann sisters took to her."

An 84-year-old Agnes Mann breathed her last in 1960. Margaret Mann died in 1966, at age 86. Only after Ada died at age 92 in 1969, did Estle Funkhouser realize how much the sisters had treasured her friendship: The Mann sisters bequeathed Crystal Cave to Estle. They left her the

70-acre tract that included their white-frame farmhouse and Honeymoon Cottage.

Estle Funkhouser kept Crystal Cave for 13 years. She was third grade supervisor at a Greenwood school, and she did her best to split her time between reading, writing and cave upkeep. Estle built Crystal Cave's gift shop. She restored the Honeymoon Cottage—replacing Alfred Mann's wicker furniture and installing a bathroom. Oddly, the cottage soon housed newlyweds—Mr. George Blower and his bride, Barbara, took up residence and worked at Crystal Cave for a time. Barbara was the daughter of a Funkhouser sister and granddaughter of William Funkhouser for whom the cottage was built.

Estle inherited Margaret Mann's dogs. Over the years, the youngest Mann sister had adopted every stray cur that appeared on cave property. Estle found a favorite among Margaret's pets in a large, hunting dog named Spot. She let the lumbering pup lope after her on excursions into the cave and confessed to the press that Spot was great company. Still, the responsibilities of running a show cave weighed heavy on the third grade teacher's shoulders.

"My sister was here by herself," points out Edith Richardson. "And care of this cave is too much for one person. Her health started to fail. So she wrote Loyd and me a letter and made us an offer. At the time, Loyd had already taken early retirement. We were situated."

"I'd been running a junk and antique store in Wichita, Kansas," Loyd Richardson adds. "Suddenly, we had to hold auction sales and yard sales to get rid of our merchandise. But when we got a chance to buy this cave, we went ahead and bought it."

Loyd and Edith Richardson bought Crystal Cave in 1982. Today they continue the cave's laid-back tradition of treating guests like they've known them for 20 years.

Edith remains Crystal Cave's primary tour guide. She still identifies cave formations with names coined by the Mann sisters: Tobacco Drying Barn, Miniature Grand Canyon, Lincoln Asleep. Lucky folks find Edith willing to show old photos she keeps behind the gift shop counter, including a photo of the Mann sisters' sign: *Stop. Honk Loud for Information.* "That was attached to a huge tree in front of the house," says Loyd. "That tree got hit by lightening. We had to cut it down."

At 80 years of age, Loyd continues to open new sections inside Crystal Cave. He labors at his work alone, removing fill shovel full by shovel full— bucket after bucket. Loyd personally stripped and replaced every inch of the cave's 1932 electrical wiring. Until a few years ago, he hunted secret passages reportedly discovered by Alfred Mann. Loyd clearly adores the time he spends underground.

"We work all the time, but we like it," Loyd says. "Crystal Cave is still a true mom-and-pop operation. When we first opened, we charged five dollars admission per person. We still charge five dollars today. There are no colored lights in the cave or anything like that. There won't be as long as me and my ancestors have anything to say about it.

We just offer folks the opportunity to see a cave in its natural state. And we let them go through at a pace they can enjoy."

Inside Crystal Cave, Time puts up its stone feet, wraps itself in cool lichen and fluffs 50 years under its head. Tomorrow, nothing will change here.

And tomorrow is eons away.

Immediate below: Alfred Mann's homemade concrete roller, designed to pack down the cave paths.

Bottom: Loyd and Edith Richardson, Crystal Cave's current caretakers.

Above: All that glitters—Mullen's 66 Rock Shop nuggets. Inset: Jim Mullen sells the stony stuff.

Mullen's 66 Rock Shop

ounce for ounce, few objects can make a heavier claim to permanency than a good old-fashioned rock. Rocks were the first toys God tossed from his playpen, and they've pebbled our galaxy ever since. Through their hefty history, rocks have catapulted at castles, skipped off caliphs' heads and barreled down alleys at armies of puny pins. They've split into Davids and fig leaves and fjords, bedecked brides' fingers and crushed the candy corn in the bottom of Charlie Brown's trick-or-treat bag.

Rocks talk bluntly to people. Their directness earns a respect not afforded wimpy trees. Ask a spelunker why he must make the dunk, and you'll get an answer better grunted than sung. The melody of the rock is the melody of machismo. Indiana Jones understood this. If the Von Trapp family really wanted to climb every mountain, they would have dropped the *Do-Re-Mi* and tuned up at a tractor pull.

Along a stony slab of Oklahoma 66 heaped high with mining history, the late guidebook writer Jack D. Rittenhouse once paused with pen in hand. The year was 1946, and men had long ceased wearing loincloths and leaping through trees. But as Rittenhouse stood scribbling beside his 1939 American Bantam coupe—recording for posterity the rocky road show before him—perhaps even he felt an urge to pop a bone through his nose:

Commerce is a town composed chiefly of homes of miners, whose cottages and shacks are mingled among the many chat heaps. In the town, where US 66 makes a sharp turn, is a large mineral specimen shop, selling samples of native and other ores for 10¢ and up.

"My grandpa was a miner," Jim Mullen explains of the Rock Shop's genesis. "And anywhere you mine around here, you'll find crystals and minerals. You find crystals and minerals, and you get collectors and geologists wanting to buy 'em. My grandpa got to bringing up calcite to sell to those kinds of folks. That's how my family got into the rock business."

Carbon dating of Mullen's 66 Rock Shop has never been attempted. Suffice to say, the family tree from which it rose has long since fossilized.

The Rock Shop itself can best be described as a Phillips 66 Station afflicted with large, awkward lumps. Its yard looks like a Cretaceous candy box brimming with blue glass and lead squares, amber insides and calcite crystals slopped atop free-standing Model A axles. Time appears to stand still here, and time to hear stories is what one finds the moment they tumble onto premises.

"After my dad married my mother," Jim continues, "my grandpa talked him into going to gather calcite. It took two guys—one stayed on top to hoist out the rocks. My grandpa gave my father a part of the rocks they gathered as payment, and my father—he had them setting outside the house, and somebody stopped and bought four or five dollars worth of them. Well, that was a lot of money back then. When my father went into the service station business, he decided to sell rocks as well. In 1934, he started in that old Marathon station up the street—on the old alignment of Route 66. Around 1940, he moved over here."

Jim Mullen spends most of his day below his baseball hat's oily brim. One of two Jurassic heirs, he and his reticent brother Ralph run the Rock Shop and the Phillips 66 station that stands at its center.

Air supply seems to mandate movement as Jim turns deliberately between cash register and car engine, quartzite and credit card machine. He sounds as sooty as Jimmy Stewart inside a coal bin—and as gregarious as Fred Flintstone hitting pay-dirt. It's a wonderful life. In Bedrock.

"Hi, Jack," goes the greeting. It's dusty and musty and meaty with moss.

"Hi," says the customer: a lanky, leathery fellow with legs that bite the ground like two drill bits.

"What can I do for you?"

"I owe you $7.15 here. Let's write the check for $50. I'm broke this morning."

"This guy," Jim explains in a stony aside, "he's been around here for about a hundred years. Or however old he is."

"I've been here eighty-five years," says the customer in jeans.

"And you're a Seneca?"

"Me? I'm Eastern Shawnee."

Jim cracks open a roll of quarters. The petrified pack doesn't easily split, and he hammers the log several times before coins dribble into the register. The tinkle of two-bits bleeds into the cry of the service station's bell, screaming another customer's arrival. "I've got to inspect this car," Jim says and rappels dutifully into the depths of the garage.

Like two prehistoric plates pinching out a dandy new diamond, the rock shop's combination service station/quarry creates a one-of-a-kind gem. This rock shop is a haven for male relaxation—a nirvana of nuggets and gritty he-men harping about weensy catches of catfish. The Chicago Bulls score high here. As do accounts of bow-hunting and any subject you can squeeze into a box of King Edward Cigars. But while engine belts strangle the ceiling—and

Gene Stanley and Joe Howard are stone-grown sages to the road weary.

The Rock Shop's Neolithic yard—still the best place to buy boulders on Route 66.

glass cases packed with stones bully each other for floor space—there exists overall a thin crust of politeness unbroken. Topics too offensive bungee jump backward before hitting rock bottom. This is a classroom of the old school. And the overgrown students are in session.

"I started coming in here about a year ago," local Joe Howard admits from under cover of his coffee cup. "We've got a group that comes in usually Mondays through Friday, you know, and there's about seven of us. And we just kind of toss it around."

"We solve the problems of the world," boasts local Cobb Wallace.

"We *pick* on one another," Joe corrects. "It's whoever's in the barrel that day."

The ceremonial circle at the Rock Shop's core assembles on yellow-cushioned chairs arranged in a sloppy half-moon—and meets regularly. This consistency seems important to all sitters. In-house pecking order is established in direct ratio to time served on one's rump. Stories told here invariably contain a healthy dose of community history. Few of these fellows have no connection to the mines that once freckled the local landscape. All of them will tell you what it has meant over the past 50 years to be a small-town American male.

When Rock Shop sitters aren't throwing stones at each other, they take turns leading visitors through the two-room specimen house in the Rock Shop's back lot. There the personal rock collection of Jim's father hunkers under lock and key. And although neglect sticks thicker than brown sugar—and warnings of fiddle-backed spiders precede any permission to enter the premises—the gems gathered from a lifetime of collecting still strike exquisitely at the eyes. Stacked towering on shelves like sandy Dagwood sandwiches, or tucked behind glass in shades of deep earth and black, each and every rock has been placed as a marker of community pride. The prevailing aroma pulls nostrils through the floor and treats them to wonderfully wet and soily places. Affixed to one wall, an article from *Oklahoma's Orbit* dated Sunday, November 10, 1963, survives. Now crisping yellow, it sings old miner's praises to the original Mr. Mullen and his Ore-Nate Eyeful.

Photos of marcasite, rose rock and butcher-knife flint decorate the story and explain how the collection grew to majestic proportions over 35 years.

"A lot of this stuff came from out in Oregon," says tour-guide-of-the-hour, Gene Stanley. "Jim's dad would cut it in two and polish it. Then he'd put it in his tumbler. He spent his lifetime collecting rocks. And when he died, he made Jim and his brother promise they'd never sell the collection in this building.

"Time was, there were plans to build a Mickey Mantle Museum here in Commerce," Gene goes on. "There was talk of putting this collection in there, but then the museum was never built. Now, nobody

Inside the Rock Shop's specimen house, stones collected over a lifetime find sitting space. Most of the specimens came from the Picher-Commerce area. Others came from farther afield. "Our spheres came from a fellow who was from South Dakota," says Jim Mullen. "He was a wheat farmer, and rocks were his hobby. He used to come down here in the winter time, when he didn't have a lot of work to do. He'd sit and visit, and we'd trade rocks with him."

knows what will happen to it when Jim and Ralph are gone."

For a moment, Commerce and Mullen's 66 Rock Shop stand honestly still. The shaft of light that squares the open doorway of the small, two-room specimen house looks yellow and crinkled and old. Skipping along in noontime sunlight, the shrill service station bell ricochets its way across time, mixed with Jim Mullen's voice behind his counter—still trying to squeeze conversation between car inspections—and the voice of Joe Howard lobbying lively against just about everything, including the coming and gentle good night.

"I told Jim and Ralph if they'd get rid of the rocks and get some domino tables," cracks the sarcastic Joe, "we could turn this into a real nice place for us old dudes."

When words and reason flake away, Mullen's 66 Rock Shop of Commerce, Oklahoma, exists as a simple celebration of age. Forget the fact this service station has pumped petrol for a rough 70 years. Forget the fact the lumps in its yard once served as a dinosaur sidewalk. Something very human rolls alongside these boulders. Hope hits hard when the common man looks calcite in the eye. Hope for long years without weakness, and inspiration to keep concrete upper lips in the face of one's own inevitable interment. Eventually, of course, tombstones will mark plots and bodies will soften to sand. But before both, the wiser fellow finds an appreciation for the simple things in life. And nothing is simpler—and stronger—than a rock.

Among the rubble and gemstones of the specimen house at Mullen's 66 Rock Shop—and all but forgotten under years inched quiet as graveyard dust, a dead sheet preaches. The placard belonged to Jim Mullens' father:

I wish I was a little rock
Setting on a hill
Doing nothing all day long
But just a-sitting still!
I wouldn't eat, I wouldn't sleep
I wouldn't even wash
I'd just set there all day long
And rest myself by gosh...

Above: Seeing stripes: Aleene and Russell Kay buy a zebra for their Buffalo Ranch at a Springfield, Mo., livestock auction. Aleene rides the beast. Russell wears a winning grin between the zebra's ears.

Left: For years, tiny Bobo was one of the biggest draws at Buffalo Ranch.

Buffalo Ranch

spirit of the circus skips down Route 66 in northeastern Oklahoma. Something wanting cymbals and a drum roll when it walks. Stepping out of Kansas, it slices through a curtain and spreads an open hand on a road of prodigious delights. Here sunbaked gargoyles dance through Dust Bowl towns. Murals tattoo Quapaw, and Commerce wears a mantle to a man, a ball and bat. Near Miami, two surviving stretches of single-lane "Sidewalk 66" wiggle across the land like halves of a rubber man's mustache, snakes jumping from jars or tightropes stretched and sagging after years of traveling toes. Approaching Afton, one almost expects an old ringmaster to appear—graying but game after a half century of service—floating a straw boater seductively westward and singing nasal vaudeville to summon round his crowd:

Buffalo gals, won't you come out tonight,
And dance by the light of the moon?

Spontaneously, it seems, Buffalo Ranch springs from the carnival air. A combination Trading Post, Western Store, Chuck Wagon Barbecue and Dairy Ranch, its four buildings edged boldly in black and yellow rear off the plain like giant sunflowers—or plastic posies—rigged and ready to squirt. Geese honk and gaggle around a crashed and splintered stagecoach. Ducklings blow by like peeping confetti. The marquee bison hulk behind fencing, sipping from bathtubs that serve as their wet bars. Buffalo Ranch is a place of weight machines and stuffed wart hogs, red plastic swimming pools shaped like Mickey Mouse and Lilliputian fire hydrants labeled "Dog Restroom." Taken as a whole, it resembles most a delirious big top that's watched its own canvas float away. Look heavenward and you might spy the blown tenting—acrobats fouled in its rigging—sailing toward Texas and points unknown.

Aleene Kay Albro, owner of Buffalo Ranch, sits inside the Western Store. The air conditioner whirs, and the air drips a pleasing potpourri of leather and boot oils, but Aleene sits impatiently straight-backed. "My purple sun glasses," she repeats. Her second husband, Leo, searches the store for the misplaced spectacles—around the boot boxes and the large trophy elk that once bugled proud and alive in the back lot menagerie. The light from the expansive dirt parking lot blasts through the windows, but Aleene blinks it aside and fixes her gaze serenely on the horizon. "Isn't this a wonderful country?" she asks.

The show must go on.

At 5 foot 2 inches, Aleene Albro is not a tall woman. The sofa from which she entertains is fashioned of steer horns tipped black, and for a moment, she looks lost and frail against its sharp silhouette. But as she speaks, she proves height can hide in a voice. Aleene Albro's words have boot heels. They walk with gritty authority. And they willingly meet anyone in any arena when the clock chimes high noon.

"Just wonder what ya do with yer bison when yer ready to get rid of the stock," drawls the rancher. He's just barreled his way through the glass door and past the sign that reads *Boots or Nothing*. He's cocky and well-fed, with a preceding potbelly and cheeks stuffed with beef jerky. In a previous life, he might have been called Hoss.

"We don't do anything with them," Aleene answers.

"You just keep 'em?"

"When they die, we have a dead animal truck haul them away."

A ten-gallon pause.

"You don't sell *any* animals?"

"No," Aleene answers.

"We sell out our calf crop every year."

"I've had up to a hundred head. And even with that many, if I had to get rid of some, I wouldn't sell them to anyone who was going to kill them."

The rancher stands confused. He stops chomping jerky, and his eyes lope suspiciously about the boot boxes. Somewhere, someone makes a fool of him; of that, he's certain. But it can't be this weensy woman in the purty black dress. It simply *cain't* be.

Aleene daily plays part in such comedies. Live buffaloes, it seems, attract wranglers like flies, and it's the rare cowpoke who passes Buffalo Ranch without making a bid for breeding stock. Aleene well understands her animals' marketability. Buffalo Ranch has thrived serving a smorgasbord of bovine dishes since its beginnings. Aleene herself frankly calls buffalo meat delicious. "But," she emphatically adds, "the buffalo here have never been butchered." Her animals are raised as pets. Meat bought elsewhere fills the bill of fare.

The Buffalo Ranch story began one warm and woolly day in Greensburg, Kansas. Aleene and first husband Russell V. Kay were welcoming tourists to the World's Largest Hand-Dug Well when they looked at each other and decided they needed something else to do. "We didn't have children," Aleene explains, "and we knew a lot of people who had never seen buffalo. So we dreamed up the idea of Buffalo Ranch." Prudence tempered ambition, and the couple scouted four locations—including one in Nebraska—before a traffic count map landed them east of Afton, Oklahoma, on Route 66. Aleene and Russell bought seven head of buffalo from a Texas breeder and raised the ranch's first building—the Buffalo Ranch Trading Post—on a budget of five thousand dollars. The year was 1953.

"We had to work hard at it," Aleene says of the first seasons. "We built as fast as we could afford to." Russell took to the tourist trade like a calf to mother's milk, and soon three additional buildings broke the Oklahoma sky. Russell and Aleene built the Western Store to sell quality western wear, and they raised the Chuck Wagon Barbecue and Dairy Ranch to stuff stomachs. Russell always hoped to serve buffalo cuisine. When roasting whole quarters of bison proved wasteful, he turned his attentions toward hawking that saucy frontier finger sandwich—that smoky bite of open prairie on a bun—the buffalo burger.

"Most people think it isn't buffalo," admits Betty Wheatley of the West's most novel patty. "It's a really good meat." Wheatley has run the Dairy Ranch for 39 years. Today she leases the building from Aleene and continues to scoop, ladle and flip old favorites like Buffalo Chip ice cream and Frito Pie. On this particular afternoon, an operatic rooster positions himself under her ordering window. He clearly comes to sing for his supper.

Left: Aleene Kay Albro began life as Aleene Karns. She began her career as a professional model. Here she poses in an Alaskan seal coat for Cownie Furs. "They'll keep you warm as toast during winters of extra walking" claimed the Cownie ad.

Above: Betty Wheatley, the buffalo gal flipping buffalo burgers at Buffalo Ranch since February 20, 1959.

Below: A gaggle of geese march on the Dairy Ranch.

"We sell just as much food as we ever did," Wheatley persists over the pint-sized Pavarotti, "but the way people eat it is different. It used to be standard, mustard, onion and pickle—maybe some catsup. But now: Everybody wants mayonnaise. They want plates with their Coneys. We still do everything like we did a hundred years ago. And we want to keep it that way."

Wheatley remembers the heyday of Buffalo Ranch, when dances by Native Americans caused cars to line Route 66 for blocks in both directions. The performers lived in tepees on the property—in partnership with Russell and Aleene. Hats were passed and all stoppers steered toward the open arms of Buffalo Ranch. Aleene often joined in the bally-hoo. In short shorts and long ponytail she stood on a stump at the corner of the property and warbled show times and hard sells over an outdoor P. A. system. A man with a stuffed buffalo, a stuffed donkey and a stuffed Brahmin bull solicited the crowd, hoisting tots atop the mounted monsters for a quick nickel and an even quicker snapshot.

Nowadays, folks return to the ranch bearing those photographs. They point to themselves at age two, or they wander out to pasture in search of an old, shaggy friend. "But animals are just like people," Aleene reminds. "They only have so much time to live."

When Aleene lost Russell to cancer in 1963, people said Buffalo Ranch would fail. Years later, the Will Rogers Turnpike bypassed the ranch, and the voices of doom loomed again. On both occasions, Aleene took the proverbial bull by its best business horns and battled back. She built a boot room onto the Western Store and stocked it with stompers stitched of rattlesnake and boa constrictor.

She welcomed country music star Freddy Fender and comedienne Pearl Bailey. Or she found and bottle fed a new baby brute until it stood strong on its own four feet.

Poachers have broken her heart. Deer are found butchered and beheaded for their antlers, and the trophy elk that now winks sleepily from its place in the Western Store was gunned down gangland-style in its pen. Too often, Aleene suffers these atrocities unavenged. Occasionally, circumstance grants favors, and justice follows swiftly on hoofed or feathered feet. Such was the time a teenager plucked the plumage from a peacock, skin and all. The Oklahoma Highway Patrol—by coincidence on the

Above: Marlene Reynolds stands at the entrance to the Indian Dance Arena at Buffalo Ranch.

Right: Two of the last Indian war dancers at Buffalo Ranch pose for this photograph taken in 1963.

The stuffed animals at Buffalo Ranch—owned by an independent concessionaire and designed for picture-taking.

property impounding buffalo burgers—apprehended the picker and brought him to Aleene for sentencing. Aleene noticed the young Yank had tresses to shame Samson. "I want his hair," she said without batting a lash, and chopped the boy's locks for the quills he'd pulled off the bird.

In spite of such incidents, Aleene has no regrets spending life as a buffalo gal. Now 75 and ready to retire, she hopes to find a buyer for her long and woolly legacy. Aleene cautions would-be whipper-snappers to learn the lessons buffaloes teach. Few animals, for instance, capture grace with such ungainly head starts. Born with oversized noggins, buffaloes nonetheless keep clouds in perspective. A common spirituality rests on their brows, a sense of community Aleene might call heart for the herd. "If you don't like people, stay out of business," she states flatly in case anyone misses the message. "If you don't like people, stay out of life."

Without fanfare, Leo returns. He can't find Aleene's sunglasses. The rancher, spotting a man, thinks to take things from the top.

"Hello there," he drawls at Leo. "I's just checkin' what ya do with yer bison when ya get too many of 'em."

"Oh." Small look at Aleene. "She told you, didn't she?"

"Yeah." Nudge, chuckle. "She said she keeps 'em. Makes pets out of 'em."

No humor. Straight-faced: "Yeah. That's about right."

Again the reply hits the rancher off guard. He reels and tries to recover, but Leo, finished speaking, disappears. Aleene rises and follows after Leo. She offers the cowpoke a consoling smile, but he doesn't take it. He's too busy staring at his size 39 boots—they look increasingly like clown shoes—and wondering who threw that well-packed cream pie.

At the Dairy Ranch, the old rooster begins another aria. The day draws near sunset, but this bird wears no watch. He's played this circuit since he was a chick and understands the demands vaudeville makes.

Somewhere in the Western Store, Aleene Albro still looks for her sunglasses. The sun creeps meekly through the windows to apologize, but she pays no attention. There are animals to feed and audiences to entertain, and she'll never stand accused of missing a curtain call.

Not while the ringmaster sings.

Buffalo Ranch often booked outside acts. One of the best remembered was that performed by Larue Olson and his trained buffalo, Pat. "Larue Olson rode his buffalo in Kennedy's Inaugural Parade," says Betty Wheatley. "He was here for two summers. Out by the Buffalo Ranch sign, he and his buffalo, Pat, would put on a show several times a day." Larue Olson strongly maintained a buffalo "could be trained but not tamed." Eventually, his words proved prophetic: Pat, the trained buffalo, killed Larue Olson.

Aleene and her second husband, Leo Albro, a few months before Aleene's January 1997 death. Today, the Buffalo Ranch remains closed and for sale. Betty Wheatley and her husband, Jim, continue to operate the Dairy Ranch.

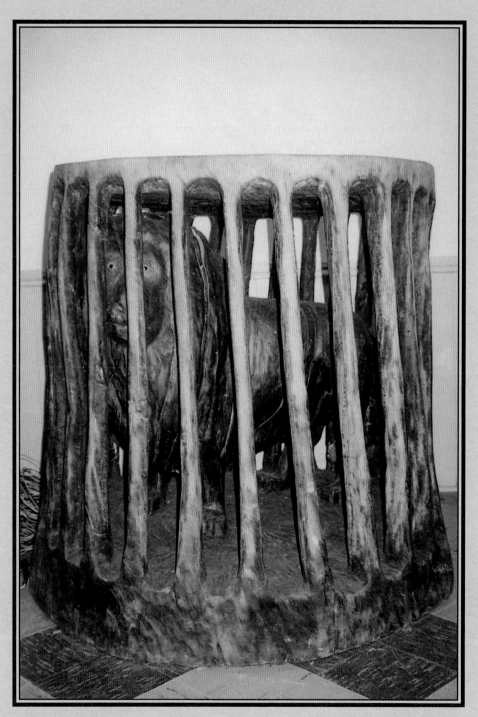
Ed Galloway's sculpted lion as it appears at its Springfield, Mo., zoo.

Ed Galloway's Totem Pole Park

The multi-dimensional mind of a sculptor is a difficult thing to finger. Ask Venus de Milo. She's been trying to get an artful grip for years.

"This is Ed Galloway's early work," says unofficial spokesperson of the Kansas Grassroots Art Association, Ray Wilbur. "Turn of the century; Springfield, Missouri." Wilbur shows interested eyes an old photograph—an enormous wood carving of a woman strangled by a snake. "Galloway's sister-in-law modeled for this sculpture. Why he wrapped her in snake, we don't know."

Sometimes, it seems, bickering beavers with Ph.D.s should punch tickets at the entrance to Ed Galloway's Totem Pole Park. The sculpted wonderland that rests four miles east of Foyil, Oklahoma, upends sensibilities that well. Across its artistic acres, turtles sprout 90-foot totem poles, fish flop atop concrete tables, and birds stick like Velcro to a tree that could have been planted by Dr. Suess. Patterns crawl inside the eye like centipedes on painted feet. Over all, four Indian chiefs stand noble in the sky, proving that Ed Galloway—the man of many faces—always had another easel up his sleeve.

Ed Galloway—and a hand-carved string section—inside the Fiddle House at Totem Pole Park.

Ed Galloway was an artisan from the first time he picked up a pocketknife. He was born in 1880, in Stone County, Missouri. He sharpened his carving skills as a child, fashioning mother-of-pearl buttons and wee, woody knickknacks. In 1898, Galloway enlisted in the U.S. Army. He traveled to the Far East during the Spanish-American War and tripped through Nagasaki watching woodcarvers at work. His art ever after contained elements Japanese.

In 1904, Galloway rejoined the civilian population. He married Villie Hooten and set up a woodshop in Springfield, Missouri. Tree trunks became his materials of choice, and he chopped fanciful sculptures from them, stitching human torsos to the tails of fish. Sometime during these early years, Galloway completed the sculpture that he forever called his favorite: an African lion behind cage bars—carved from a single wood block.

"Mr. Galloway was making carvings in Springfield for the Exposition in San Francisco," says Galloway's daughter-in-law, Joy. "One day, his

shop caught fire. The fire burned everything he'd made for the Exposition except one piece. That piece survived because Mr. Galloway kicked it out the door. If you look at the piece today, you can still see the nicks that the bricks of the pavement made on it as it rolled down the hill."

In spite of his workshop fire, Galloway decided to attend the Panama Pacific International Exposition. He took his surviving sculpture—a 29-foot reptile wrapped around a sycamore tree—and loaded it onto a westbound train. In Tulsa, Galloway stopped to visit friends and find money. He housed the sculpture in a drugstore on Archer Street. Sand Springs philanthropist Charles Page passed by the store window and saw the wood carving. So taken was Page with the carving's craftsmanship that he appointed Galloway manual training teacher at the Charles Page Home for Widows and Orphans.

Galloway's career at the Charles Page Home cut across two decades and uncounted acres of trees. The woodshop over which he presided functioned as

Ed Galloway with a few of his early tree-trunk sculptures—including his infamous snake and sister-in-law piece. Galloway's treatment of his sister-in-law apparently caused her no harm. Today, she remains alive and well in an area rest home at the age of 105.

a commercial factory. Boys were taught to build tables, tools and wagons. Ever the artful master, Galloway made certain he stretched young minds. He continued to carve sculptures from tree trunks during off hours—much to his students' delight.

In 1934, Galloway attempted retirement. The Sand Springs Home called him back in 1935, but in 1937, he finally wiggled free. Galloway moved with his family to a tiny farm east of Foyil, Oklahoma. There he began construction of an ambitious retirement project: a tribute to the American Indian filled with concrete sculptures and totem poles. Galloway called this wonderland Totem Pole Park.

Totem Pole Park showcased the tallest totem pole in the world. Galloway built the massive, 90-foot centerpiece over 11 years, exhausting six tons of steel, 28 tons of cement and 100 tons of native sand and rock. A man of modest means, Galloway concocted his own cement mixture. He hitchhiked into Claremore and Chelsea and combed lumber yards for scrap materials.

"Mr. Galloway had always made totem poles," Joy Galloway says today. "People have forgotten that. At the Sand Springs Home—when a tree died in the yard around the woodshop—he would take out his tools and carve the tree into a totem pole. He would make something beautiful out of it, and leave the dead tree where it stood."

Galloway built his big totem pole one floor at a time. He hand-plastered mortar over a steel and wire skeleton and designed 200 carvings in the damp cement. He completed painting and other finishing work as he went. Galloway hoisted himself by pulley to higher levels and worked while sitting in a small swing. Near the totem pole's top, Galloway placed four 9-foot carvings of Indian chiefs—among them, Geronimo, Joseph and Sitting Bull.

"Here's an early version of the finished big totem pole," says Ray Wilbur, pointing to another photograph in his album. "In this version, the totem pole has an arrowhead at the top, and the four Indian chiefs are free-standing. Later on, Galloway went back, took the headdresses off the Indians and made the totem pole taller. He couldn't stop building."

Galloway topped his big totem pole with a long timber—at the tip of which wavered a weather vane. Sources say Galloway added the post to make his totem pole taller than any other in the world.

Galloway planted smaller carvings in the shadow of his giant. He constructed a concrete fish table complete with scaly chairs for picnickers. In 1957, Galloway built his birdhouse—a Dr. Suess-like tree that provided summer homes to purple martins. Galloway worked on these creations as much as 16 hours a day. Evenings, he retired to his dining room and whittled wooden fiddles—scraping them with broken glass as he sat beside his stove.

"The fiddles were really a wood collection," says Joy Galloway. "The goal was to carve one fiddle from every kind of wood in the world. Mr. Galloway had a brother who was a great violinist; I believe that is why he chose to carve fiddles. Although few—if any—of Mr. Galloway's fiddles were ever strung, some of them were lavishly inlaid."

In all, Galloway carved nearly 400 fiddles. Each fiddle was numbered, and each fiddle carried the name of wood from which it was carved. Galloway finished many of his fiddles during World War II, a windfall that helped him acquire wood from faraway trees. Boys he had taught at the Sand Springs Home were now grown men scattered over the globe. A monthly newsletter sent to them carried Galloway's request for exotic materials. Galloway's old students responded, sending their teacher *raoi* wood from Hawaii and mahogany from Siam.

Galloway's hobbies took a toll on his marriage. Villie Galloway well-weathered her husband's construction of Totem Pole Park. She accepted with less grace house floors swimming with wood shavings. But when Galloway day after day dragged strangers into their home under pretense of showing his work, Villie drew her own artistic line. "She told him, 'I'm tired of people in my house,'" Joy Galloway says. "And so he built the Fiddle House."

Galloway constructed his eleven-sided Fiddle House on the east side of Totem Pole Park. He first called his showplace the Grape House for the fruit clusters (and occasional tree frog) carved into its support beams. Murals decorated walls; wood-relief pictures looked out at the world through pieces of white balsam, dark cherry and black teak. Along the back and one sidewall, Galloway hung his fiddles.

"I don't charge a nickel for people to see this stuff," Galloway told reporters. "I like them to stop and talk and enjoy seeing it. That's worth more than money." For those who insisted on making a contribution, Galloway set out his Monkey Jar—a glorified receptacle that swallowed pocket change. Registered guest books recorded more than 400,000 signatures.

To the east of the Fiddle House, Galloway gave "Little" Joe Holman a parcel of land on which to develop a business. The young Foyil man built a soda stand the size of a chicken coop—and grew it into a grocery with gas pumps. In time, Totem Pole Park became Foyil's community center.

Galloway kept carving.

"Mr. Galloway got an awful lot of his information from *National Geographic* magazine," says Joy Galloway. "In fact, he ordered 9-by-12 pictures of every president from Washington thru Kennedy. He made wood portraits of all of those presidents, using different colored wood for hair and facial features. He even put glasses on Harry Truman.

"He was hanging these portraits in the Fiddle House when he fell. We took him to the hospital, and the hospital discovered he had cancer."

Ed Galloway died in 1962. Shortly after his death, thieves kicked down the doors of the Fiddle House and stole many of Galloway's fiddles, wood carvings and all of his presidential portraits. Galloway's family moved the remaining woodwork into the home on the property. The home was subsequently ransacked.

The park itself slowly succumbed to fits of wind and weather. Color sloughed off the totem poles, and the roof of the Fiddle House collapsed. Totem Pole Park looked all but lost when the Kansas Grassroots Art Association rode out of the Sunflower State and

The Wizard of Arts: Ed Galloway.

into a partnership with the Rogers County Historical Society to save it. In 1983, volunteers began clearing brush. For roughly a decade, volunteers twice a year camped at Totem Pole Park and mounted another artistic push to reclaim what time had taken. Sparrow hawks lodged in the old birdhouse fought every reclaimed inch. Those restoring the big totem pole worked from one color photograph and tiny flakes of paint clinging to the concrete.

Today, Ed Galloway's Totem Pole Park stands fully restored. The Fiddle House again functions as a museum, and 15 of Galloway's surviving hand-carved violins hang in their former showplace. In a Springfield, Missouri, zoo, Rogers County Historical Society members found the sculpted lion that Ed Galloway called his favorite work. They hope to bring the kitty home to complete Ed Galloway's Oz.

"In one lifetime," Joy Galloway muses of the whiz that was her father-in-law. "To accomplish what Mr. Galloway did in one lifetime—I still can't imagine. His work is all over Sand Springs.

"So much of his work was simply incredible. The daughter of the first boy to graduate from the Sand Springs Home has the sculpture I like. If you're familiar with Totem Pole Park, there's a picnic table with chairs there covered with fish. This friend has a dining room set like that—made out of inlaid wood. During the year that Mr. Galloway retired and moved to Foyil, his son—and my late husband—Paul Galloway was a senior in high school. Paul wanted to graduate in Sand Springs with his class. So he stayed with these people. Mr. Galloway made the furniture to pay for Paul's board. Fifty years ago the worth of that table was estimated at $10,000. Baseball players with the St. Louis Cardinals have tried to buy it for their clubhouse."

IMPRESSIONS OF TOTEM POLE PARK:

Top, left: The big totem pole.

Top, right: A speckled gecko.

Center: A school of Galloway's scaly best.

Bottom: Concrete critters climb the birdhouse.

Mendenhall's Bath House, the first establishment in Claremore, Okla., to smell money in radium water.

Radium Town
& the Will Rogers Hotel Baths

We have all kinds of various "weeks"—"Eat an apple week," "Don't shoot your husband week," "Don't cuss the Republicans any more than you can help week."

But, Claremore, Okla., the home of the great radium water, is having this week one of the most practical and useful ones, "Take a bath week." Even the Rotarys, Kiwanis, Lions, Apes, and Chamber of Commerce have joined in the novelty of the thing and it bids fair to become a yearly event.

—Will Rogers

Claremore was a city of wet miracles. The faithful knew this the moment they made town. Claremore's borders smelled bad, and that was good. Men wrinkled mustaches and ladies lowered kerchiefs to sniff the stench that rose to the nose after banging its way through pipes city-wide. The punch the air packed was proof positive Claremore ran rampant with healing radium water. For more than seven decades, swarms of the sick, the weary and the waterlogged wobbled into town to topple into tubs—led by pipers who plopped into the stew to pickle their own peppers.

The tale of Claremore's miracle baths began with the discovery of the fusty water that filled them. By the early 1900s, homes nationwide were dumping coal furnaces in favor of heaters fueled by oil or natural gas. The trend inspired Claremore businessman George Washington Eaton to form a company to bore into the ground. On May 15, 1903, Eaton sank a well on his property—and hit a gusher.

Early eyewitnesses said Eaton struck oil. But nostrils on site smelled a stinky rat. *This* bubbling crude smelled rude and abusive and appeared too thin to fuel anything. Closer inspection confirmed Eaton had hit sulfur water—and hit it hard. Within a week, workers were grumbling that the water's stench burned their eyes. Neighboring newspapers began printing poo-poo jokes. "The prospecting well at Claremore has only reached a depth of 1200 feet," the *Vinita Chieftain* cracked. "The hot water is rushing out like mad, boiling and seething while the sulphurous fumes rise. The reckless citizens threaten to drill on 400 feet more, evidently bent on being taken into and made a part of Greater Hades."

If the Devil was selling real estate, he was dead set on offering waterfront property. A sea of sulphur water drowned Eaton's pasture. Houses hit by the spray saw paint and metal burned black. Frogs and turtles took one taste and expired.

But mammals, surprisingly, appeared to benefit from the bad-smelling brew. Some say a pup was deliberately dipped in the deluge; others insist a dog was incidentally doused, but all accounts agree a mangy mutt came into contact with the water—and began sprouting frisky new fur. One of Claremore's more courageous citizens filled a tub with the water, submerged himself in it and lived to tell a pleasant tale. By June of 1903, a modest bathhouse operated on Eaton's property. The *Claremore Daily Progress* felt secure enough about the situation to aim a small splash at town critics. "Those that try the baths speak highly of them," the paper reported, and crept meekly away in search of a towel.

No serious move toward commercialization of the water occurred before February of 1904 when a sample was sent to Washington University Professor of Chemistry, Edward H. Keiser. The game professor broke out his beakers and shoved in his nose plugs and said, "I find this water to be highly charged with hydrogen-sulfide gas. This is the same gas that is present in the waters of Sulphur Springs, Virginia, and other famous spring waters. It has medicinal properties and is valuable on this account."

Entrepreneurs aiming for Claremore began packing rubber ducks. One of the first to arrive was Dr. W.G. Williams of Quincy, Illinois. Williams hoped to build a sanitarium in Claremore, and he asked the Claremore Industrial Company to lease him the artesian well. The Board drew up a contract, but pulled the bath mat out from under the good doctor's togs a few weeks later—announcing it would sell the well to William Perdue and associates for $1,500. The resulting Perdue Bath House became a Claremore civic jewel. Locals and visitors alike frequented its long sitting porch. Horse-drawn taxis whinnied up to all Claremore trains to trot bathers to the Perdue.

Mendenhall's Bath House—the first bathing hut built on the Eaton property—continued its booming business at 25 cents a dip. The venerable tub room would in time become Claremore's longest-lived spa, rebuilt at 7th and Lavira as a two-story brick structure, and renamed Keller's Bath House. The area around Mendenhall's became known as Radium Town, a gurgling city almost unto itself. The name derived from the widespread belief that Claremore's reeking water shocked bodies with a healthy dose of radioactivity. Advertising brochures fed the folly by showing bodies emanating auras. Apparently, those who took the waters at Claremore not only felt great but glowed in the dark, too.

Dr. E.E. Lacy was a chiropractor who operated Lacy's Bath House in the heart of Radium Town. "Always an atmosphere of friendliness in pleasant surroundings," promised Lacy's 1953 ad. The bath house attracted guests with weekly rates, full meal service and a "Television-Lounge-Reception Room" in which to "while away the time."

Claremore's therapeutic pools never attracted the bathing elite drawn to tubs in Hot Springs, Arkansas, or Sulphur Springs, Virginia. A large percentage of Claremore's customers were elderly, and the city patted itself on its well-washed back for offering quality water treatments without pricey frills. Nevertheless, in 1923, city leaders launched a one-quarter million dollar drive to build a community bath house fashioned after the spas in Hot Springs. When the drive fell short, the bath house was built anyway—as the somewhat smaller-than-planned Radium Bath House. The Radium Bath House never had adjacent living quarters for patients. Although its facilities matched or excelled any in the city, lasting popularity eluded it. In the middle 1950s, the Radium Bath House found itself closed and for sale, even as spas like Lacy's and Bennett's—and tub departments at the Sequoyah Hotel, the Bungalow Hotel and the Will Rogers Hotel—whipped themselves into a wealthy froth.

The Will Rogers Hotel threw itself into the mineral water pool on February 7, 1930. Three men—Louis Abraham, Walter Krumrei and Morton Harrison—had conspired to make the hotel the tallest building in Rogers County. The six-story structure boasted 78 rooms and seven apartments and sported Spanish decor in imitation of Will Roger's Santa Monica home. Bellboys met baggage around the clock. A coffee shop sliced famous cinnamon bread. Opulence boggled all eyes—except those that lingered on the hotel's linens.

"The water in Hot Springs, Arkansas, as I understand it, is not dark," says Louis Abraham's daughter, Luanda Doffer. "Some days the radium water at the Will Rogers Hotel would be very dark. One lady said she wouldn't stay at the hotel because she didn't like the dirty linen. Well, the water had stained it. However elegant the hotel was, it couldn't keep its sheets from looking dingy."

The Will Rogers Hotel Bath Department sat in the hotel's sixth floor penthouse. Architect Krumrei placed his tubs on the top floor for privacy's sake, but lived to regret his decision. More piping meant more leaks. Claremore's mineral soup chewed through steel like a liquid lion.

Bathers making the long journey into the clouds found the Will Rogers Bath Department split into two distinct halves—one side soaking women and the other stewing men. The water, which shot cold from the ground, was heated to an average of 102 degrees. Bathers began treatments with a 15-minute stint in a steam bath. After their half-hour tub time, they were wrapped in blankets, consigned to a cooling room and finally finished off with a massage—often at the hands of Levi Harlin.

Levi Harlin started work at the Will Rogers Hotel in 1942. He was the fifth masseur hired on the men's side of the bath house, and he took the job at a starting salary of $14 a week. In all, he would knock knots out of bodies for more than 50 years.

Levi was a native Oklahoman who had learned to bend bodies at a chiropractor's side. He believed passionately in the curative powers of Claremore's water. This faith—combined with his remarkable massaging skills—made Levi a bit of a bone-bending legend. Customer after customer came to the Will Rogers Hotel Bath Department seeking the attentions of Levi Harlin. Spas in Hot Springs, Arkansas, actively courted him. Patti Page found peace under his palms. Senators counted on Levi for soothing slaps to their backs.

In Levi's day, the public's thirst for Claremore's water bordered on mineral mania. The earthy tea was touted as a cure for everything from eczema to alcoholism and dandruff to neuritis. Soakers signed up for series of water baths that often lasted several weeks. Braver water bugs found faster ways to get the good stuff home.

"People would drink the water," remembers Levi's son, Levi Harlin, Jr. "The Will Rogers Hotel sold the water in one gallon bottles. Then, they used to have what they called a colonic. They'd run the mineral water through your rectum. Not too many people took to those."

Eventually, Radium Town and the Will Rogers baths began to succumb to the day of the fortified vitamin. In 1976, Pearl Golden and husband, Russell, purchased a much quieter Will Rogers Hotel. Levi Harlin was still smoothing muscles, but now he was the last masseur on premises.

OPEN DAILY
8 A.M. - 8 P.M.

MEN'S   DEPARTMENT   •
MINERAL WATER BATHS
Sixth Floor

BATH   1²⁵
MASSAGE 1⁰⁰

The Will Rogers Hotel Bath House, where the elite came to soak sore bones. Levi Harlin stands front and left.

In the middle 1980s, the Will Rogers Hotel saw public interest in mineral water revive. The baths drew as many as 20 people a day, all seeking natural ways to beat stress. But the resurgence was short-lived. Levi Harlin wrung a final neck or two, and the Will Rogers Hotel closed in 1991.

Radium Town's last spa had drained dry in 1980.

Remnants of Claremore's bath industry survived. In January of 1994, the Rogers Country Historical Society purchased the abandoned Will Rogers Hotel. A $2.5 million restoration project evicted pigeons, refurbished the hotel's lobby and turned old rooms into senior housing. On the hotel's sixth floor, three of the bath house's bone-dry tubs were preserved.

In Radium Town, Keller's Bath House was converted to apartments. Lacy's Bath House was demolished. On site, a few stark gray tubs remain to this day—beached in a field among shards of broken tile like fading and oar-less rowboats.

Levi Harlin spent his remaining years working down the street from the Will Rogers Hotel. He ran the Steam Room at the Best Western Will Rogers Motor Inn. There, he continued to show sore bodies who was boss. Levi forevermore massaged without the wonderful water in which he believed. When friends called seeking it—and they frequently did—Levi was forced to tell them that Claremore had run out of miracles.

At age 74, sick, and in the hospital before his March 1996 death, Levi Harlin still entertained visits from the mineral faithful. Senator John Wilkinson came to see Levi one day. The senator shook his head over his old friend and masseur and professed his belief for all the bathers who had ever found wet comfort in Claremore.

"Levi," sighed the senator, "if we had that water now, you wouldn't even be in here."

Faith is an ingredient too often missing from life's daily drudge. If one reason exists to undertake any journey, that reason involves finding something in which one can believe. Many roadies revisit Route 66 desperately seeking a Fountain of Youth. Some travelers are not disappointed. But wiser drivers find comfort knowing the old road offers simpler wonders—if not a place to walk on water, at least a room in which to soak sore feet.

REMNANTS OF RADIUM TOWN:

Left: A few crumbling tubs meet the light of day on the site of Lacy's Bath House at 9th and Lavira streets.

Below: Mendenhall's/Keller's Bath House was the longest-lived tub room in Claremore. Closed in 1980, the building has since been converted to apartments. The sign remains.

Above: Call me Moby. The Blue Whale as
it appeared in the autumn of 1996—before
its new coat of turquoise.

Right: Everywhere one looks, baby blues
haunt the Blue Whale grounds.

Wolf Robe's Trading Post, Nature's Acres & The Blue Whale

ood things come in small packages. Whimsy requires more elbow room. The anniversary gift Hugh Davis built for his wife, Zelta, was born of a romance as big as the ocean blue. "I loved animals," Zelta Davis remembers. "Hugh wanted to give me the biggest animal there was. And so, he gave me the whale."

Unless motorists ride submarines down Route 66, odds say they'll butt up bumper to blowhole with the smiling Blue Whale of Catoosa, Oklahoma. The 80-foot cetacean—created of cement and sucker pipe—has been a whopping area landmark for almost 30 years. Modern road books by everyone but Captain Crunch have arguably made the Blue Whale the most popular icon on Route 66. Schools of grinning tourists come to stand in its gullet and snap pictures. Oklahoma governors drop by to re-dot the pupils in its eyes. So popular, in fact, has this lovable lubber grown that history has all but forgotten the whale was built as a private offering of the heart—a beach-side bouquet with a tail—and a token between two people who understood we share more with this world's wild things than the occasional sardine.

The lifelong safari that Hugh and Zelta Davis traveled together began among the cages of Tulsa's Mohawk Zoo. Hugh Davis was a seasoned Jungle Jim. He was considered an animal expert long before he became zoo curator. Hugh had trounced through Africa for two years, filming baboons with famed wildlife watchers Martin and Osa Johnson. He'd scampered up stages too numerous to mention to chatter about chimps or chimpanzees. Hugh's wildlife writings seasoned *National Geographic*. His nature photographs prowled through the pages of *Life* magazine.

Zelta was a fair-weather farm girl who had spent summers in the country and winters in the city—courtesy of her father's work schedule. Her mother far preferred the place where she could dig in the dirt, and she raised her daughter to fear nothing that crawled out of God's ground. Once, when a blue racer appeared inside the family mailbox, Zelta's mother took pains to teach her daughter that snakes—and other animals—were people, too. This lesson proved invaluable the day Zelta married Hugh and found her life wrapped around the charming beastie boy—and the box of animal crackers that necessarily came with him.

Hugh Davis, African explorer.

"There was a baby mountain lion that was caught out in New Mexico by a banker from Chelsea, Oklahoma," Zelta remembers. "It took two men and a cowboy to wrap that thing up, and they shipped it here—to the Mohawk Zoo.

"When it arrived, Hugh took me out to look at it. I felt so sorry for it because it looked scared to death. I told Hugh, 'I think I can go inside the cage with that cat.' And he said, 'Honey, they just caught it out of the wild. That thing will tear you to pieces.' Well, I've always had a way with animals. So I went into that cage, and I talked to that cat, and it didn't offer to eat me alive. The next morning, I dressed formally. Hugh took a picture of me holding that cub in my arms. They used that photograph on the front page of the *Tulsa World*.

"Back in Chelsea, the banker opens up his paper that morning and here's a picture of some idiot woman holding the cat that it took three people to subdue. He almost had a heart attack. I got a call from him on the phone. He thought I was just about the bravest little woman in the world."

Above: Zelta Davis wears a foxy stole.

Below: The Davis family at one with Nature. From left, Dee Dee, Zelta, Hugh and Blaine.

Hugh himself learned his bride was more than a match for any beast. Annually, the Davises traveled to Okeene, Oklahoma, to lead the town's Rattlesnake Round-Up. Photographers from *Life* magazine would follow Zelta into the field. On banquet night, Hugh gave a reptilian lecture. Zelta served as a slithering prop, entering from auditorium's back with snakes wrapped around her neck. Grown men, startled by her attire, jumped onto tables and dashed through dishes and food. Old ladies took one look at snakes nibbling Zelta's fingers and fainted dead away.

Hugh and Zelta's experience with tickling a nation's travelers began in partnership with Hugh's brother-in-law, Chief Wolf Robe Hunt. Wolf Robe maintained a trading post at Tulsa's 11th and Harper Streets during the days Route 66 called 11th Street its own. He was a full-blooded Acoma Indian, a renowned silversmith who supplemented his own stock of jewelry creations with those fashioned by his two brothers back in New Mexico's Sky City. Each year, Wolf Robe returned to Gallup to display his wares at the Inter-Tribal Indian Ceremonial. He typically traveled with the Davises. "Hugh and I would camp with the Navajo Indians," Zelta smiles. "Wolf Robe would stay in a motel."

About the same time Hugh and Zelta bought property near Catoosa, Oklahoma, Wolf Robe looked for a new retail location. The two families joined forces to start a new store near the Davis home. Called simply Indian Trading Post, the high-quality craft store was owned and operated jointly by Hugh and Wolf Robe until a new alignment of Route 66 sliced the Davis' property in two. With traffic suddenly behind their home, Hugh and Zelta decided to sell their interest in the trading post to Wolf Robe and build something beastly across the street.

"All my life, I loved alligators," Zelta explains. "So I told my husband, 'Let's develop the land over there into an alligator ranch.' He thought I was crazy. 'You can't have alligators!' he said. I asked him, 'Why not?' and he said, 'Well, alligators are a lot of trouble.' I told him I could handle that trouble, but he said, 'Honey, let me just build you an ark. You can give children's birthday parties, and we'll have cut-out animals, and we'll scale everything to the children's size.'"

Chief Wolf Robe Hunt was not only a renowned silversmith, but co-author and illustrator of the book, *The Dancing Horses of Acoma*.

The Ark—the first flight of fancy to land on the Davis' property—was a success. Concocted complete with on-board, cut-out animals, its tables and furnishings were built to pint-sized scale. As Hugh predicted, the Ark scored well with parents looking for a place to hold children's parties. Unforeseen were the number of adults who wanted to board the boat as well—bumping their heads and coming out bruised. Fortunately, Zelta continued to hound Hugh to develop some type of attraction for big kids. At length, Hugh dug a couple of ponds on the property, and Zelta got her gators as well.

Today, Zelta admits she wasn't completely prepared to care for her toothy, cold-blooded wards. Although she'd spent time spoon-feeding strips of liver to little snappers at the Mohawk Zoo, full-grown gators were another matter.

The alligators themselves—with the exception of a 14-foot-9-inch male named Gulliver—frolicked uncaged among the property's ponds. Footpaths tied the terrain in bow-knots. Zelta conducted tours along these trails—taking the lead on the way in and bringing up the rear on exit to insure hungry mouths followed no one home. Once, while leading a tour, Zelta took an alligator nip to her leg. On another occasion, she nearly became a tidbit for big Betty.

"Betty took me to the water one day, but it was my fault," Zelta insists. "I was feeding the alligators chicken. They love chicken, and it makes your hands nice and soft.

"When they see a bucket, they know you've got food. And you learn not to feed all of them until you just about finish your trail 'cause they're right behind you, following like a bunch of ducks. Betty had eaten well that day. She had gone down to the water and was lying there with her head up. To my surprise, she decided she wanted another bite to eat. She lunged after the chicken, and she got my hand.

Above: Blaine Davis and son, John, inspect the toothy inventory at Nature's Acres.

Below: Zelta Davis pets Betty, the large alligator that almost made her into a meal.

Hugh Davis was once the recipient of an onstage rattlesnake bite. Unflustered, he had the wound slashed and its poison extracted in front of his horrified audience to demonstrate proper first aid.

"Well, I knew I couldn't open that mouth. So I went to the water with her. As soon as I got her in the water, I hit her on the end of the snout. When you do that, an alligator's mouth will typically open. I got my hand out, and I got the heck out of there. And Betty just looked at me as if to say, 'What's wrong?' She didn't intend to bite me. I'm sure of that. But I had to get my hand stitched up, and I was awfully glad I'd learned that snout trick handling gila monsters over the years."

Hugh and Zelta called their wild kingdom Nature's Acres. Locals simply called it the Catoosa Alligator Ranch, although alligators were never the only animals displayed. Nature's Acres contained a prairie dog village. Two snake pits pocked the property, one stocked with poisonous snakes and one that Zelta had fashioned as a playpen for her grand-children. "My grandson, Paul, would give his own little snake shows in there," Zelta says. "Little girls just love that stuff."

Frequently, guests slipped into Nature's Acres' one gator-free pond for a quick swim and cool-off. The practice frightened Zelta who felt certain a drowning loomed in the wings.

The Davises solved this problem in the later 1960s—shortly after Hugh retired from his position at the Mohawk Zoo. Zelta took a job at the Travel Information Center at the end of the Will Rogers Turnpike, and Hugh assumed charge of Nature's Acres. Hugh quickly decided the gators should go. He hauled them to Hope, Arkansas, and released them into the swamps. Nature's Acres became a proper swimming hole charging 50 cents a dip.

"The kids kept saying, 'Mr. Davis, we need something to jump off of,'" Zelta explains. "Then Hugh had Harold Thomas over there—a friend of ours who was a welder. They started putting pipe into the lake. Hugh knew exactly what he was going to build, but he wouldn't tell me. If I questioned him, he'd just smile and say, 'I'm working on it.'"

The 80-foot icon that would arguably become the best-loved landmark on Route 66 began as a twinkle in a retiree's eye—and took two years to complete. Hugh was 70 years old when he began building the Blue Whale. He worked from his own plans and lugged concrete up ladders five pounds at a time. This last chore was no small feat: As Hugh aged, he suffered greatly from crippling arthritis.

Above: The Blue Whale during construction. Note the hole left for the water slide and the eye already in place. The young carpenter is John Davis.

Below: The Blue Whale in all its briny glory.

"When he got it finished, it was the Whale," Zelta says simply, "and he gave it to me as an anniversary present. And then the debate was, 'What kind of whale should we have?' Everybody said, 'Oh, make him a *mean* whale—make him black and white.' I said, 'We don't have mean things.' So we made him a friendly, blue whale."

Swimmers boarded the Blue Whale through its mouth and tiptoed across wooden planking. Water slides shot from the whale's port and starboard. A spigot flowed from the whale's blowhole and kept slides slick. Inside the whale's head, a ladder led to a loft riddled with portholes. Diving boards sprang from its tail. The Blue Whale wore a red, plastic bubble hat—a cap fashioned from a piece of junked jumbo jet. At night, the hat glowed and gave passersby the impression one of Boeing's best had plopped into the pond.

Hugh and Zelta prided themselves on keeping their swimming hole family-friendly. At the Blue Whale, alcohol was not allowed, neither was sand-throwing or swearing like a sailor.

Guests signed in at the time they arrived. Three to five lifeguards watched tykes at all times, and a concession stand served thirsty kids. Canoes were available for rent. Fishing was permitted from the side of the lake opposite the whale. The pond was stocked with perch, bass and channel catfish.

Hugh moved two boats onto the property and into permanent dry dock. One was a large boat that afforded adults sunbathing space. The other was a boat for children covered with cut-out sharks, groupers and an octopus. The Boat of Education—as this second vessel was christened—contained blackboards on which kids could scribble. Hugh tacked the alphabet on one side of the boat and numbers one through ten on the other to prepare little skippers for school.

In a prominent place on the grounds, Hugh erected an elaborate, hand-carved totem pole. The intricate, four-sided column proved to be his final tribute to the wildlife he loved. Painstakingly, Hugh covered its sides with whittled animals and birds. "After all the years of caring for animals, I decided that's the best kind to have," Hugh told local newsmen. "They don't eat, and you don't have to carry a scoop shovel around after them, either."

As years passed, the popularity of the Blue Whale never waned. When the swimming hole closed in 1988, it closed due to Hugh's declining health. Hugh Davis died in January of 1990.

Modern day visitors to Catoosa find the Blue Whale sporting a fresh bucket of bluewash. In 1997, the Catoosa Chamber of Commerce orchestrated efforts to refurbish the fabled landmark. Oklahoma Governor Frank Keating himself arrived to repaint the pupil in Moby Dick's eye.

Hugh's Ark and other pieces of Nature's Acres were not part of the refurbishing project. Today, they bob like wreckage above a sea of weeds.

Zelta Davis continues to live where she's lived for so many years. Her life remains rich with images of animals—from the miniature whales slip-sliding inside a soap dish to panels from Hugh's totem pole that adorn her walls. Davis family photos are menageries in themselves. The Davis children, Dee Dee and Blaine, came of age wrapping pythons around each other like wiggling lengths of jumprope.

They often shared beds and bath times with adopted animals. Bongo—a black bear cub—and a grizzly named Geyser came to live with the Davises after suffering problems with their own parents. No stronger evidence exists that Hugh and Zelta Davis considered all creatures family.

"Bongo loved pickled peaches," Zelta laughs. "He'd sit in my lap and eat them like they were going out of style."

Centuries from now, if one remnant of the Route 66 amusement world remains, the sentimental sailor hopes the holdout will be the Blue Whale of Catoosa, Oklahoma. On the sea of imagination, the smiling leviathan certainly earns its keep. But in quieter, human waters, the whale makes its most heartfelt splash. This baby blue trophy will always stand as a monument to all husband and wife teams along Route 66—and a spouting love letter between two particular souls who walked hand-in-hand onto shores unexplored and found this world's wild things not so savage after all.

Zelta Davis today.

Crystal City scenes: From top to bottom, the Zingo Roller Coaster, the Loop-O-Plane and the Crystal City Sqintorium.

Electric Park
& Crystal City Amusement Park

Inside his booth along the midway, X marks his spot.

Too bad X can't remember the rest of his alphabet.

Amnesia wraps his brain in a forgetful rubber band. Street number, home state and his own proper name have long since sunk beyond recoverable reach. Truth be told, X can't remember his favorite food. Although Johnny tells him it must be a vegetable called cabbage. Johnny says X makes the money.

Another customer comes forward to play the carnival game. X does his job, answering questions and smiling a lot. "Could your name be Nathan? Nolan? Nelson?" The words enter X's skull and ring up triple zeros. No sale. No dice. No cigar.

Over the creek and beyond the swings, the sound of music begins. X relaxes in spite of the contestants in his face. X has been over that creek to peek into the sideshow tent. He's seen the Human Caterpillar. He knows that fellow can't remember where he left his own limbs.

"Cuba? California? The Casa Loma Dance Hall?"

Someday, X thinks, his princess will come—a woman from nowhere will recognize something and drag him home to people who will give him back his name. On that day, X knows, a jackpot will be paid, and Crystal City Amusement Park will lose one of its most profitable attractions.

Until that time, X marks the man.

Senses short-circuit at amusement parks. Salted as heavily as midway peanuts, they crash into each other, intoxicating their riders and burning out reason in bursts of bravado, puppy lust and crocodile tears. The situation is one born of the automated age. Before the dawn of mechanical monsters built to whip, flip and torture our fragile human frames, fun was but a rowboat ride—an afternoon spent drifting through life's placid pools. Early-day amusement meccas commonly catered to this quest for serenity. From Coney Island's Sea Lion Park to Detroit's Belle Isle to Electric Park in Tulsa, Oklahoma, the focus of fun was on water— and the many things one could ride through it.

"Electric Park existed long before Crystal City Amusement Park," says Tulsa's Marvin Peters. "A creek ran through the property, and they dammed it up at the south end of the park where it ran under the railroad. They made a little lagoon, and they had canoe rides there. That was the big deal. Then, of course, Electric Park built one of the biggest swimming pools in the state. I worked at Electric Park as a locker boy."

Electric Park was born in olden days of old-time ways, in an age when the wattage from the common bulb still amazed. At night, couples strolled through the park to ooh and ah at its brightness; daylight found sweethearts snuggled in rented canoes or metal rowboats. In the shallow end of an enormous pool, swimmers dog-paddled their way through lazy Sundays, dodging the frequent diving competitions that marked the deeper waters. Even the famous wrestler Ed "Strangler" Lewis was sucked in by Electric Park's wholesomeness. Between meets, the beefy bruiser spent days entertaining pint-sized fans at the swimming pool's north side where a large sand area sat.

"'Strangler' Lewis used to come out there and lay around," says Marvin Peters. "Us kids would wrestle with him. He was a big old guy—a world champion—with big, cauliflower ears. But he was just a puppy to us." As Tulsa grew older, Strangler's tradition would stick. Around Electric Park's venerable pool, wrestlers Leroy McGuirk, Ralph "Wild Red" Berry and "Gorgeous George" Wagner would all take good-natured turns kicking up grit.

In the middle 1920s, William Falkenberg decided to develop land adjacent to Electric Park. He founded Crystal City Amusement Park—an amusement mecca that would in time outshine and absorb its older neighbor.

Falkenberg was a wealthy businessman who enjoyed his role as a dandy. He built a two-story home—at the time considered the snazziest two-story in the county—immediately across the railroad tracks from his new enterprise. "Falkenberg was a tall, slender man, and he was probably 55 or 60 years old when I first saw him," says Marvin Peters. "He had a Cord automobile—a real luxury for the time. Once, he picked two or three of us kids up going toward town—just to show off. He drove about 60 miles an hour in that Cord. We thought we were flying."

Flying was specifically what Falkenberg had in mind. From the beginning, Falkenberg bet his bankroll on making Crystal City the biggest and the best amusement park in Oklahoma. He cast an early eye on Tulsa's Sunset Park, and its wooden roller coaster. Falkenberg decided he would build his park around the largest roller coaster Oklahoma had ever seen. His designers brought him the Zingo on a screaming silver platter.

Words still stick in the throats of survivors who rode the Zingo. The frenzied concoction of bracing and slats did stand taller than any coaster the Sooner state had seen. At night, electric lights pocked its bony frame. By day, the Zingo became a scribble of bellyaches and blurs. The press gave the Zingo the attention of a new national weapon. So tall and imposing did its ribbing stretch that it blotted out attractions beyond, leaving everything but Crystal City's central tower hidden to those standing outside the park's pearly gates.

Falkenberg complimented the Zingo with a number of secondary rides and attractions, including a batch of circus acts designed to terrify observers. The best of these played near the park's center, where a daredevil regularly scaled the tall tower to take a swan dive toward a teensy tank. Splashdown after splashdown proved successful until the day the diver missed the tank. His would not be the last life Crystal City would take.

Crowds mobbed Crystal City in the park's early years. Marvin Peters remembers Route 66 clogged with pleasure seekers in 1928. The traffic never thinned until the Depression dawned, and, then, Crystal City began a slow dance for survival. The mighty Zingo closed and stood silent as a rotting snake. Rides vanished from the park. And William Falkenberg went on his way.

"When I bought this park, it was only 13 acres in size, and there were no rides," Johnny Mullins would one day remind the Tulsa newspapers. "It now covers 27 acres. We have about 15 major rides in the park, and seven more for kids."

In 1937, Johnny Mullins seemed Crystal City's perfect savior. A natural-born showman with a saber-toothed sense of the absurd, Mullins could wring dimes—and entertainment—from a washcloth. His purchase of the park in 1937 brought Crystal City back from bankruptcy and ushered in the park's grandest years.

To a greater degree than Falkenberg, Mullins invested in old-fashioned sideshow attractions. At the back of the park—and accessed by footbridge—a sideshow tent stood. Separate admission was charged at the tent's entrance, but a peek behind its canvas brought lookers face-to-face with some of the most famous human wonders of the day. There the Human Caterpillar—born without arms or legs—performed feats with his mouth. There local talent, Joan Whisenant, went through her musical paces.

"Joan Whisenant was born without arms," says Tulsa's Ben Bishop. "I went to school with her younger brother. She was a fascinating lady. I used to see her driving the streets, and there were articles in the paper showing her changing her baby's diaper using her toes. Her act was playing the steel guitar with her feet."

Out on the midway, an amnesia victim sat in a gaming booth. Mullins offered money to anyone who could help the forgetful soul recover his memory. Eventually, a girl from Kansas claimed the man and took him back to parents in the Sunflower State, but not before the contest made Mullins a mint.

Mullins took great care to improve the Casa Loma Dance Hall. The exquisite arena sat southwest of the park proper. Over the years, it had grown from a tiny, wooden shack into a formidable nightclub. Mullins positioned a canopy over Casa Loma's outdoor terrace. He painted the canopy with celestial bodies, and advertised "Dancing under the Stars." On sweltering Tulsa nights, Casa Loma's country and western music could be heard for miles.

Crystal City enjoyed its most successful years in the early 1940s when 15,000 people could daily pack the midway. An Octopus, Tilt-a-Whirl and kiddie jungle ride added in 1943 helped pad the park's thrill bill. One day, a car on the Loop-O-Plane broke loose during routine operation. A couple was thrown free and killed. The event signalled the beginning of the end for Crystal City. After World War II, Mullins became intrigued with the new medium of television. He began buying broadcasting stations. In 1948, he sold Crystal City's rides.

Mullins retained ownership of the Crystal City property. He kept the Casa Loma Dance Hall and the old Electric Park swimming pool open for business. By this time, the pool had installed its own waterworks system and a filtration plant adequate for the needs of a small Oklahoma community. On any given morning, diver Henry Phillips dove into the pool's deep end to vacuum its insides. His efforts were no substitute for Mullins' neglect.

"The last time I was out there, that pool was a mess," says Tulsa historian, Beryl Ford. "It was not safe. It didn't meet the code, and it was rougher than a cob. I think the pool eventually closed simply because it wasn't attractive anymore—unlike the Casa Loma Dance Hall."

The Casa Loma Dance Hall stumbled forward until 1950 when it became the last piece of Crystal City to close. Over the next five years, parts of the park flared in mysterious fires. By late spring of 1956, no evidence of fun remained.

Mullins and partners W.R. Grimshaw and Don Nix opened Crystal City Shopping Center on the site in 1959.

Today, Crystal City Amusement Park exists only as a phantom—an imp that sits on shoulders of older Tulsa residents and whispers of a place that once smacked senses silly. Typically, Tulsans that remember Crystal City recount it in remarkable detail. In spite of the park's dubious standing as the first major amusement park to die on Route 66, Crystal City tingles nostalgic nerves more than most. When Mullins closed the park, visitors approached him begging to buy particular swings on which they'd kissed their sweethearts. In 1968, Robert Kiwanis Bell built Tulsa a new Zingo roller coaster inside Bell's Amusement Park. Bell had come of age riding the Crystal City classic. He remembered something worthwhile in Tulsa's glittering park.

A busy Crystal City day in 1928.

"My father took me to Crystal City when I was a young boy," says amusement man, Bobby Bell, Jr. He made me ride the Ferris wheel. I remember I was scared to death. My mother was mad at him for making me go. But, for some reason, he thought that ride was good for me."

Visit Bell's Zingo. And while you're clacking toward the clouds, consider how a simple day in an amusement park can stick with one for decades. Think how your own town's roller coaster measured your summers and your youth. Think hard on your ascent, and try to find your answers before you top that first big hill.

Odds say you're a blathering idiot on the roaring ride down.

Above: Harry Hayes' roller rink at Dixieland Park. Daughter Jo Ann and playmate roll out the smiles.
Below: A teenage Jo Ann and skating date scoot past a Dixieland casualty.

Dixieland Park

I n Sapulpa, Oklahoma, the glory of the rink never sinks into the sunset.

The arena for the agile, the well-wheeled and the clumsy stood outside city limits—six miles by the gage of travel writer Jack D. Rittenhouse. Part of a larger complex, the roller rink shared its surroundings with a swimming pool of Olympic proportions. Cabins waited to rest legs weary from turning laps or lazy eights, and a man named Buxton manned a meaningful restaurant—shoveling salmon and jumbo shrimp into Oklahoma mouths. Over all, a private plane puttered. On the facade of every large building, the letters loomed, spelling out for customer and confederate the park's enticing name—Dixieland.

Says Sapulpa's Jo Ann Haag, "In the 1920s and 1930s, there was no other place like Dixieland. Not in the state of Oklahoma. Not in the surrounding states. Dixieland was that unique."

The rise of Dixieland Park began, appropriately, in the deeper South. Clyde Hayes and his brother, Harry, were simple country boys, farmer's sons sweating in the fields of Bentonville, Arkansas. Love led Clyde to Oklahoma—his in-laws lived in the oil-rich town of Sapulpa. And after the courting was complete and wedding knots knit, Clyde found himself running a grocery alongside his father-in-law, Joseph Grooms. But Joseph Grooms was a man of vision—a former railroad engineer who had seen the country's insides and kept his eyes peeled for

The service station at Dixieland Park.

money-making trends during trips down the tracks. One day, he took his son-in-law aside and told him: A man could find a fortune owning one of those new-fangled swimming pools.

Clyde marked the old man's words. In August of 1927, after Grooms had passed away, Clyde closed the grocery and formed a partnership with friend Earl Townsend. The partners bought 40 acres of property from land baron Max Meyer and set out to hew a swimming hole into the side of Route 66.

Max Meyer himself had stretched a timid toe into the highway trade. Down the road from the land he had sold to Clyde and Earl, the temperamental tycoon maintained a string of tourist cabins. These cabins inspired Clyde to design Dixieland Park as a full-service facility. One-room, stucco cabins would stand at a distance from Dixieland's pool. A gas station and a cafe would take turns filling tanks.

Clyde dug Dixieland's marquee swimming pool on a mammoth scale. Sixteen artesian wells filled its 100-by-150-foot frame with shimmering blue. An adjacent kiddie pool served swimmers of shallower age, and an immense bath house provided plenty of room to change trunks. Showers were required of all swimmers. Small, medicated pools took hard stuff off heels.

Clyde's daughter, Edna May Hayes, poolside.

"The swimming pool had a high-diving board, and the water in that end of the pool was 18 feet deep," says Jo Ann Haag. Belly-floppers shied away from the plank in the sky, but professional divers came to Dixieland specifically to try its springs. One was Johnny Weissmuller. The Olympic-swimming-hero-gone-Hollywood-Tarzan was well-practiced in plunging from high places and delighted in taking Dixieland's drop. No one knows if he worried for his coconuts on the way down.

Dixieland Park offered picnickers grounds filled with barbecue pits, tables and swings. Clyde's wife, Hazel, grew fragrant rose gardens. Locals came to Dixieland just to smell the blooms. A miniature golf course challenged putters. But for all the park's perks, Clyde felt Dixieland needed something more. He began talking to his brother, Harry, back in Bentonville.

"Clyde had got his land out there in Oklahoma and started with the pool," says Jo Ann Haag, "and then he began talking to my dad about coming to Sapulpa and doing something. At the time, my dad was working for the Frisco Railroad. Like Clyde's father-in-law, Joseph Grooms, he'd been all over the country. I believe it was in St. Louis that my dad had seen a roller rink."

Harry Hayes and his wife Lorene moved to Sapulpa in 1928. The same year, their daughter Jo Ann was born. The couple bought ten acres of land adjoining Clyde's property. They squeezed their growing family into a Dixieland tourist cabin while Harry built a home—and a roller rink.

From its outside, Harry Hayes' roller rink looked like an airplane hanger. Inside, fine-fitted maple made up its floor. A bandstand sheltered musicians from dive-bombing bodies. A sitting area served skaters who landed on their rumps. Swimming at Clyde's pool cost ten cents, so Harry charged skaters one thin dime. When folks grew unruly on wheels, Harry himself became the rink's bouncer.

In the rural America of the 1920s, roller rinks were as common as accordion-playing cows. Most Sapulpa locals had never before seen one. Many came to Dixieland simply to understand the fuss. In time, Dixieland Park developed a reputation as a place where sophisticates gathered to play.

The interior of Dixieland's roller rink.

The Dixie Inn did its best to foster this fancy flavor. During the cafe's early years, Red and Donna Wilson served up scrumptious ribs and sandwiches slathered in Red's Hot Sauce. Later lessees Frank and Emma Buxton shot their dishes over a mouth-watering moon.

"Buxton renamed the restaurant the Dixieland Club," says Jo Ann Haag. "And he began serving a very exclusive menu—delicacies like jumbo shrimp and fresh salmon. Back in the 1930s, foods like that were unheard of in Oklahoma. Buxton had a fellow with a private plane fly this food in from the coast. Because he had that kind of food, Buxton began to attract dignitaries. In those days, the Dixieland Club was beautiful. It had a dance floor. You could buy almost anything there that you wanted."

Like not-too-distant Crystal City Amusement Park, Dixieland's popularity boomed in the years immediately preceding World War II. Under Buxton, the Dixieland Club lured every lawyer in Creek County to its tables. A string of senators wiggled out of Washington to sample its savory wares. Movie stars William "Hopalong Cassidy" Boyd and Gene Autry dog-paddled Dixieland's pool. Orchestras rocked the roller rink, and Miss Sapulpa Contests kept the whole park looking pretty and demure.

But five years after World War II, Dixieland began to drown in its own deep end.

"Clyde couldn't keep up with the filters that the state mandated for the pool," Jo Ann Haag says of the glitch that dragged Dixieland down. "The water was filtered constantly, but they wanted him to drain the pool—oh, mercy—I think they said once a week. Clyde couldn't do that, because he filled the pool out of those 16 wells. That shut down the pool.

"Around the same time, Mr. Buxton died of cancer. The Dixieland Club closed. My aunt and uncle made that building into a home. They lived there for quite awhile."

Dixieland Park closed in 1951. For many years afterward, Harry Hayes' determination saw the roller rink roll on as a solo act. Eventually, age forced Harry to abandon his role as bouncer. He leased and ultimately sold the rink to Buddy Stockton. Stockton kicked out the skaters and turned the rink into a simple honky-tonk. The building subsequently burned.

Today, Dixieland's bathhouse remains the last of the park's standing structures. The building houses an automobile salvage business. It retains little of the splendor of days gone by.

"I don't go out there," Jo Ann Haag admits. "It makes me too sad. The pool is still there. It's full of junked cars. But the rink burned. The house I was raised in burned. The old cabins—I guess they were bulldozed.

"Dixieland was unique. When you consider, we're talking about the 1920s. It was unheard of to have a facility like Dixieland back then. And the fact that it was built by two young brothers from Bentonville, Arkansas—that's just amazing."

Over Sapulpa, high clouds still dive. And the memory of the rink tugs playfully at sleeves—picture perfect in the sight of two people snuggled close and gliding down the street arm-in-arm. Listen carefully. You might just hear the clack of wheeling roller skates. Or the melodious song of the South itself—turning lazy figure eights—and wistfully whistling Dixieland.

Jimmy Burge, the mastermind who rebuilt the West as Frontier City, U.S.A.

Frontier City, U.S.A.

The UFO landed in the spring of 1959.

Little green men failed to disembark. No death ray baked bystanders. No demands came to be led hand-in-tentacle to trembling world leaders. Yet something about the silver spaceship bothered Doc Holliday. There the saucer sat—smack center in his frontier town. That wasn't how the West was won.

On this particular morning, Doc has dearer matters on his mind. Inside the ice cream parlor, Dusty Dan, Pecos Bill and a crew of criminal others huddle around sugar cones. Doc hates when they do that. Vanilla and Fudge Ripple do not a dignified outlaw make. Doc will see they all eat lead in the afternoon.

In front of the silver UFO, a ticket line grows. Doc drops his gruff expression for a moment to consider what the future holds. Certainly, he thinks, there are other frontiers to be found. But maybe Martians themselves would love the old west. Maybe some day they'd show up for real—wearing bolo ties on their oozing, intergalactic chests and trying their darndest to walk like John Wayne.

They'd best be law-abiding citizens, Doc thinks, and turns around to welcome the good people of Oklahoma to the streets of Frontier City.

 t some time, every American kid plays cowboy. The game comes as naturally as nose-picking and noogies, a playful rite of passage teaching lessons in pretend. Game rules are simple: whooping counts, and if you're bad, you take your gut-shot like an itty-bitty man.

Crime doesn't pay when you play cowboy.

As a wee whippersnapper, Jimmy Burge surely played cowboy with the best. Jimmy retained a pearl-handled grin as an adult, the sort of smile that suggested he still packed a popgun, and he wasn't afraid to use it. Jimmy knew that somewhere in grown psyches big boys continue to ride in chaps and plastic boots that Grandma gave them long ago. Purdy girls pined for men in white hats. And so Jimmy built a city where the good guys always won.

Jimmy's career on the amusement frontier began in Oklahoma City. At age ten, he took a job as usher at the Criterion Theater. Jimmy grew up and went to Hollywood. He worked as an MGM press agent for Joan Crawford and Robert Taylor and returned to Oklahoma City to manage the Municipal Auditorium. In 1957, he took the reins of the state's Semi-Centennial Celebration. One of the celebration attractions was a reconstruction of a 1907 boomtown replete with rustic facades and oil derricks.

Jimmy had seen Disneyland. He worshiped Walter Knott, the whiz behind Knott's Berry Farm. To Jimmy, this boomtown looked like big money and big fun. After the fair, he picked up several of the boomtown's pieces and began fashioning a permanent amusement park—Frontier City, U.S.A.

Jimmy placed his amusement park on land outside Oklahoma City—land homesteaded in 1889 by Ezra Walter Parks. From the beginning, Jimmy built shrewdly on the westbound lanes of Route 66.

"Families on the way to California will stop for every snake pit and rock pile along the way," Jimmy explained to tickled reporters. "When they start back, they've seen Disneyland and Knott's Berry Farm. They've spent all their money. They're three days late getting back to Ohio, and they wouldn't stop for the Last Supper with the original cast."

Jimmy laid out plans for his wild west town with a team of four investors. He turned the original storm cellar built by Ezra Parks into a jam and jelly shop. Semi-Centennial designer Russell Pearson drew up the town's facades.

At its core, Frontier City would be a corporation headed by Jimmy. Admission to the park would be free. Oklahoma businesses would establish mirror images of themselves inside the park—in late 1800s form—and tenants would pay part of their profits to the corporation. The plan looked fine on paper, but enticing merchants to move in was another matter.

One night at a dinner party—and in an effort to find another investor—Jimmy cornered laundry chain owner R.F. "Jack" Williams. Unbeknownst to Jimmy, Jack Williams had come to the table gunning for him. Williams wanted Frontier City's new linen rental contract. But he found Jimmy's enthusiasm contagious. Jack Williams became Jimmy's partner.

With Williams aboard, construction of Frontier City finished in a final, ten-week flurry. On May 30, 1958, and at ten o'clock in the morning, Oklahoma Governor Raymond Gary officially opened the park by shooting apart a piece of rope stretched across its stockade entrance. Oklahoma City's mayor and a band of city councilmen rode to the ceremony in an authentic covered wagon. Upon their arrival, they were met by Frontier City Mayor Jack Williams who looked a lot like the Oklahoma City laundry baron of the same name and who—by no coincidence— washed linens on-premises in a building made to look like a Chinese laundry.

"My dad was part owner of the corporation, but he was also a tenant," explains Jack Williams' son, Fletcher. "The first year, he had a division called Williams Enterprises which consisted of eight rides and attractions. He later added more. One of the attractions we had was the O.K. Gunfight Corral.

Frontier City postcard shows popular park icons, including the Burning Covered Wagon and Jack Williams' first-season '89er Ghost Mine. Today, the Ghost Mine remains one of Frontier City's few surviving original attractions.

"My dad built the Gunfight Corral because he could see people really came to Frontier City to see gunfights. The Gunfight Corral charged 25 cents. It had sound systems and lighting and all kinds of special effects. People sat in bleachers bought from President Eisenhower's second inauguration."

Jimmy Burge designed Frontier City to be a city in itself. The park boasted its own zip code, its own postmark, its own newspaper and government. A marshall and a deputy acted as a peewee police force. A small fire department put out petty fires. Reverend Russell Rauscher conducted regular services inside St. Raphael's Chapel of the Guardian Angel. The Episcopalian mission was promoted by the Williams family who had persuaded their preacher to raise funds for the holy house. Frontier City even printed its own money—with Jack Williams' face on the loony, legal tender.

The corporation managed Frontier City's train ride and staged street fights. Park promotions were products of Jimmy's runaway mind. The Burning Covered Wagon that for years attracted onlookers outside Frontier City's gate was a typical Jimmy Burge baby. The scorching prairie schooner flamed on 24 hours a day, 12 months a year.

"Our local gas company helped support the burning covered wagon," says Fletcher Williams. "They pushed up a little berm of dirt underneath it and ran the gas line through that. The wagon was made out of fire-retardant material, but it looked like it had just gone through an Indian attack. People were always stopping to take pictures of it. The wagon finally burned out in the late 1960s. I think our gas company stopped supporting the gas bill."

During Frontier City's first year, 1.3 million people visited the park. Jimmy Burge estimated attendance by counting heads on the park's train ride. In preparation for its second year, Frontier City undertook an $800,000 expansion. Twenty-six rides and concessions were added to the park. One was the 2,200-foot "Tepees to the Towers"—a cable car ride owned by drilling contractor A. Q. Haferkamp that raised 14 people in an arrow-shaped car to a 100 foot tower. Jimmy Burge and friends appeared determined to turn Frontier City into another Knott's Berry Farm.

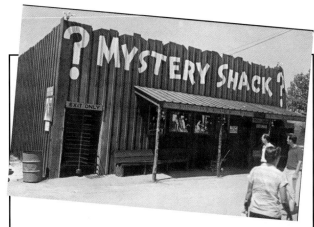

Water ran uphill and brooms stood on end inside the Mystery Shack—an early Jack Williams attraction.

Jimmy's ambition may have blinded him the day Maryland scientist Otis T. Carr came to Frontier City. Carr claimed he could build a spaceship that would physically fly to the moon. Jimmy came up with the money to fund Carr's project. The resulting OTC-XI Flying Saucer was a cosmic dud. "This guy had convinced Jimmy and a few other folks that he could build a flying saucer, and it would really take off," says Fletcher Williams. "Of course, it was a total flop. The guy skipped town.

"The saucer was eventually salvaged. They showed a motion picture inside it: You got into a chair and leaned back and saw a picture of the thing taking off to the moon and coming back. The saucer always had a line of people in front of it. People shelled out money left and right to go into that thing. But how out of place can you be? A flying saucer in the middle of an Old West theme park?

"In those days, Frontier City was unbelievable," Fletcher Williams continues. "What kind of kid would not love having a whole frontier town at his disposal? I got to wear cowboy clothes every day. My dad was the mayor. There was even money printed with my dad's picture on it. I had a little scale Model T car I got to drive around town. How lucky could I be?"

By 1960, Frontier City was billed as the most photographed spot in America. In March of that year, Jimmy Burge sold his stock in the park to Allen Dean, a theater manager from Ardmore, Oklahoma.

Take me to your tumbleweeds: Frontier City's OTC-XI Flying Saucer.

Jack Williams remained with Frontier City for 17 years. Other originals hunkered down for the long haul as well. One of the long-timers was Bob Mythen—a mustached dandy who became Frontier City's marshal—and legally changed his name to Doc Holliday.

Born in 1915, Bob Mythen was a native Tulsan with an extensive firearm collection. He worked as a reserve officer for the Oklahoma City Police Department. On his 42nd birthday, he walked into Frontier City and discovered he was destined to be a gunfighter. He and his wife, Noni, moved into a white-frame farmhouse inside Frontier City. Bob changed his name to Doc at the Tulsa County Courthouse.

Doc crafted five-to-seven-minute scripts for the park's daily gunfights. Over the course of his career, he personally gunned down 100,000 men.

Doc took an active role in hiring Frontier City's gunfighters. Dan Corley came to work for Doc at age 16. At the time, Corley was in high school in Shawnee, Oklahoma. Doc wanted Corley to grow a moustache, but Corley's school dress code forbid facial hair. Determined, Doc wrote Corley's principal a note. "So when the principal sees the note, he starts laughing of course," Corley told the *Daily Oklahoman*. "He said, 'Yeah, sure, this note came from Doc Holliday. And I'm Frank Sinatra.'" Doc picked up the phone and gave the principal a call. Corley received permission to grow his moustache.

In the heat of mock gun battle, Doc's detailed scripts didn't always unfold as planned. Once, while staging a shoot-'em-up, Doc fired on the Frontier City Bank only to see its doors shred to smithereens: A live shell had been lurking in his shotgun. On another occasion, Doc's deputy fired at close range into Doc's lower leg. Spouting much more than catsup, Doc crawled under a table in the O.K. Gunfight Corral and gamely finished the fracas.

As a matter of course, the Frontier City stagecoach fell into the hands of fine-acting bandits. In 1961, Dan Corley—who by now was called the Omaha Kid—watched a woman suffer a heart attack during a staged robbery. One afternoon, dazed stage-coach riders confronted Doc Holliday at the sheriff's office. The visitors wanted to know where they could reclaim wallets snatched during their stagecoach ride. Jimmy Burge sheepishly admitted that Frontier City robbers never took wallets. He gave each guest a fistful of dollars on condition they wouldn't go to the press.

The 1960s were not kind to Frontier City. Major fires and windstorms plagued the park, destroying the O.K. Gunfight Corral, a huge livery stable and half of Fort Street.

In 1968, Frontier City tumbled into bankruptcy. The Small Business Administration sold Frontier City at public auction to Abe and Howard Slusky—a father and son team from Omaha, Nebraska. The Sluskys added 13 new rides over the next four years and incorporated arts and crafts displays, a picnic area and a catering service. Tickets sales jumped 30 percent between 1971 to 1972. But by 1975, a third fire had ravaged Frontier City. The Lost River Ride, the Mystery Shack, the Cider Mill, the Penny Arcade and the Shooting Gallery were among the cooked casualties. Jack Williams and other long-battered tenants moved on.

In 1981, Frontier City was acquired for $1.2 million by the Tierco Group. The Tierco Group aimed to knock down the old park and replace it with office buildings. But the commercial real estate market softened, and Frontier City was given one last shot.

In 1983, amusement park wunderkind Gary Story took Frontier City's reins. Story had managed an amusement park in Sydney, Australia. He felt Frontier City's malaise could be lifted by embracing the intentions of the park's original builders. To that end, Story and park manager Manny Gonzales poured through old photo albums and journals in their attempts to understand Frontier City's history. They popped western film after western film into an overworked VCR. They made notes about gunfighters' costumes and cowtown architecture.

In the end, Gary Story and Manny Gonzales removed Frontier City's old stockade fences and gave the park a more streamlined look. They rebuilt the boardwalk and repainted the park in a new color scheme. West Texas Productions took over the staged gunfights, doing honorable fury to the memory of Bob Mythen. Patrons rushed back to boo, cheer and applaud by the tens of thousands.

Frontier City has since continued to carve notches into its fun gun. The park installed its first roller coaster, the Silver Bullet, in 1986. In 1991, it welcomed the Wildcat, a wood and steel screaming classic dragged piece by piece from Kansas City's Fairyland Park. The Nightmare Mine—an indoor coaster—and the Diamond Back were built to further rider thrills. Between the screams, Frontier City added Paul Bunyan's Tiny Timber Town, a play-ground for little choppers; the Prairie Schooner, an enormous swinging pirate ship; the white-water ride Renegade Rapids, and a nightly, seasonal $2000 fireworks show.

In 1998, Frontier City christened a new Gunfight Corral. Augmented with trapdoors and pyrotechnics, the state-of-the-art arena found Frontier City turning full-circle to its Jimmy Burge and Jack Williams days and embracing its rootin'-tootin' roots.

"This is what our dream was," Jack Williams told the *Daily Oklahoman* in 1988 as he revisited his former stomping grounds. Jimmy Burge, sauntering along, smiled his pleased pearl-handled grin. Both men seemed to see that Frontier City—that dusty, crusty cowtown that on some avenues appears to outgrow old britches—remains a place that shoots imagination sky-high. Do Jimmy and Jack the honor of catching that last stagecoach into town. You won't find a better chance to strap on your chaps, spur on your best pony and play that magical game you've been missing for the last 40 years.

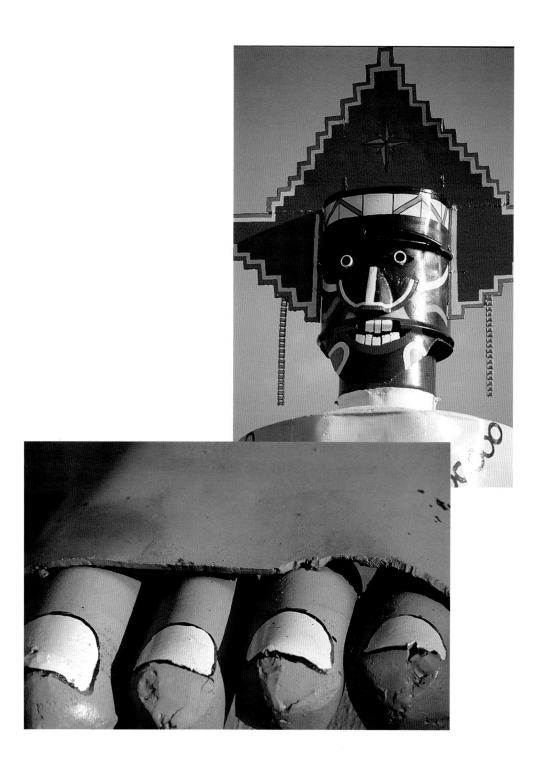

Top: Myrtle, the Queenan's king-sized Kachina doll.

Bottom: Myrtle's Johnny-come-lately toes.

Queenan's Trading Post

ooming large in a section of western Oklahoma—and in a land so short on landmarks the sun stops at 7-11 to ask directions—a colossal Kachina doll stands. It stands like Caesar unfallen, drum-bellied and broad, with a high head of laurels that crosscuts low clouds. It stands like Goliath disdaining David's slung stone, a steely Paul Bunyan scarred thickly with welds. It stands like Godzilla. It stands like the Thing; it stands like King Kong without Chiquitas and fuzz.

And it stands on feet studded with pretty, painted toes.

"The toes are ridiculous," Wanda Queenan says of the titan's prominent pigs. "Whoever heard of a Kachina doll with toes? I've never seen one. Yet, the artist who completed the restoration gave that doll toes."

Wanda Queenan well knows the inappropriateness of toes—and spats, chaps or sandals—on the heels of Kachina dolls. She and husband Maurice "Reese" Queenan owned and operated Queenan's Trading Post—that Mecca for moccasins that once stood on Elk City's west side. The restored metal giant—that today towers a Cinderella slipper's throw away from Elk City's National Route 66 Museum—once stretched above tourists in the Queenans' front yard. In those days, it donned proper boots and attracted all travelers to the best tourist stop Elk City ever saw.

"Before I was born, my parents ran a store in Fonda, Oklahoma—a store for Indians," Wanda explains. "I grew up listening to stories about Powder Face and American Horse, but I never dreamed there were such people left alive.

"After I graduated at Carter, I moved with my family to Elk City. I met my husband to be, Reese Queenan.

"Elk City is in Cheyenne and Arapaho country. Reese had many friends who happened to be Cheyenne or Arapaho Indians. After we were married, these Indians began bringing things by the house that they'd made and wanted to sell. My husband wanted to help his friends, so we'd buy things and resell them.

"Gradually, we worked our way into the trading post business."

Business for the Queenans began inside a rented building in the center of Elk City. The couple lived in an upstairs apartment and maintained the building's bottom for trading traffic.

Elk City's own trading post queen, Wanda Queenan.

Reese soon realized good money could be made selling his merchandise to merchants out west. By 1944, he and Wanda were routinely packing boxes into a spacious Chevy and puttering across the Texas Panhandle to peddle their wares. In the Land of Enchantment—from Albuquerque's Harvey House to Tobe Turpen's Trading Post in Gallup—Reese became known as the Moccasin Man.

"The Indians with whom we worked were beaders," Wanda explains. "They beaded on leather. That was a novelty to the West because the traders out there were used to nothing but pottery and jewelry and rugs. People used to ask me, 'Where do these beads come from?' And I'd tell them, 'Before Indians began trading with white men, they made their own beads from colored stones and porcupine quill. After the white man came, the Indians began using trade beads.' Good seed beads were made in Czechoslovakia."

"Eventually, we got patterns from the Indians. I would cut out the leather for the moccasin tops. The Indians tanned rawhide for the soles. The moccasins were sewn together with sinew. Everything was handmade. No machine touched any part."

In 1948, Reese and Wanda turned in their traveling shoes and anchored in Elk City. Tourist traffic had grown thick enough to permit parking in one place, and the couple bought and built on a plot west of town. They called their store Queenan's Trading Post. By 1949, functioning tepees pimpled the property, and Reese's friends were moving in.

"We had one Indian out there named Ralph Middleman," says Wanda. "He was full-blooded Arapaho, but he dressed like a cowboy with hat, scarf and jeans. He lived in one of the tepees. At night, you'd see him by the firelight beating his drum. He made German silver jewelry. Inside the store, we kept a pigskin table where he worked.

Wanda and Reese show a buckskin dress to a customer inside Queenan's Trading Post.

Left: Wanda dons buckskin. Right: Reese (called Chief Little Stink on photograph's back) on the trading post's steps.

"One day, my husband and Ralph were talking inside the store. Reese was a hippie before there were hippies—he wore braids, and you could usually find him in a vest without an undershirt. A tourist came into the store—all bug-eyed—and asked me, 'Can I talk to that Indian?' 'Sure!' I said. Ralph stood up, and the tourist pointed to my husband and said, 'No, the Indian! The one in the braids!'"

Wanda's parents, Cyrus and Florence Sanders, moved into a trailer on the trading post's property. Reese built them a cider stand called the Kickapoo Corral, and they did a fine business selling refreshments along Route 66. The receipts of Queenan's Trading Post sat comfortably in the pink, but new ideas gnawed at Reese. He believed a stronger gimmick would capture more cars.

"We'd been west," Wanda explains, "and we'd seen all these gaudy, big things out there—things like big arrows in the ground or the giant rabbit at the Jack Rabbit Trading Post.

"We knew a fellow at Sayre who was a welder. His name was Johnny Gray. His original name was Grayfish, and he was a Delaware Indian. He and my husband got together and decided they would make Kachina dolls to attract the tourists. Giant Kachina dolls. Made out of oil drums and pipes."

The first Kachina doll Johnny Gray created looked like an enormous string bean. The sculpture's head was horned, and its hands were upraised—according to Reese—as if to say "How" in greeting. Visitors might have just as easily thought the creature signalled low-flying planes.

Above: Wanda's parents, Cyrus and Florence Sanders, served cider at the Kickapoo Corral.

Below: Reese and the first welded Kachina doll.

Together, Wanda and Johnny Gray painted the first Kachina. The second Kachina was painted by a transient Indian of the Santo Domingo tribe. The "Big Kachina"—as the second monster was called— stood taller and fatter than the first. Wanda's father took one look at it and playfully named it Myrtle.

In a land plagued by cyclones, the wry Cyrus Sanders also weighed Myrtle's worth as a weather gage. "When the wind blows Myrtle's skirt up," he cracked, "we'll know it's time to head for the cellar."

Totem poles and smaller, wooden Kachinas joined the welded jumbo twins, but Johnny Gray's twosome always stopped the most traffic. Today, Wanda has no idea how many photos were taken of the Kachinas over the years—only that they brought visitors back long after Elk City's section of Route 66 was bypassed in 1971. By that time, Wanda's parents had passed away. The cider stand was closed.

Reese himself had died in 1962. Wanda—and Queenan's Trading Post—pushed on until 1980.

One finds Wanda Queenan today at her retirement job at the National Route 66 Museum in Elk City. An attractive woman who has aged gracefully, the only obvious evidence of her trader's life lies with the names of old friends that trip poetically off her tongue: Clara Coyote, Verna Yellow Cloud, Martha Finger Nail and Archie Black Owl.

"I'd like to write a book about the Indians as I knew them," Wanda admits. "Not in my folks' time. And not today because relations are different. I miss working with my old friends. Old Lucille Young Bull comes in to visit me once in awhile. Others still hunt me up—thinking I might buy something."

Wanda looks out her window and quiets. One of the best-kept secrets of Route 66 is the secret that Queenan's Trading Post never completely closed. Even today, Wanda might make a deal on her lunch hour. Her stock has dwindled, but Santa Clara black pots still stand for sale on the trading post's shelves. In recent years, the Elk City Chamber of Commerce restored the trading post's two giant Kachinas. Both now stand on the grounds of the National Route 66 Museum. Myrtle, of course, stands on those hefty, Fred Flintstone feet.

When Wanda is gone and memories of Reese shake their booty into the Elk City sunset, Myrtle will stand sentinel on the shoulder of Route 66. Shutterbugs will stop to snap pictures of her. Few visitors will think twice about Myrtle's bootless feet—or her ten prodigious tootsies of Ozymandias size that will even then await the return of the Moccasin Man. And his beautiful, beaded shoes.

Above: The Queenans' daughter, Tonia, dwarfed by Myrtle, the big Kachina.

Right: Reese in war headdress behind the trading post's jewelry case.

Below: In 1958, Reese stands next to one of the post's artful signs.

REPTILE VILLAGE, OKLAHOMA
5 MILES WEST OF ERICK, OKLA. ON HIGHWAY 66 AND I-40

In this postcard, Reptile Village rears its watermelon stand.

Reptile Village

In their wild and rattling heyday, snake pits inspired more self-righteous finger-wagging than any other breed of highway business. By virtue of cold-blooded company kept, the owners of snake pits were themselves often seen as scaly things with forked tongues, evil imps who stabbed receipts on barbed tails and tucked those tails into underhanded pants. To many locals, befriending pit people was akin to babying Beelzebub. Some towns treated their snake folk with open animosity. In Alanreed, Texas, citizens dropped dead asps on the grounds of the Regal Reptile Ranch, hoping to harm the ranch's reputation and send its owners slithering shamefully away.

Remarkable, then, in herpetologic history does the story of Billie Henderson lie. A cobra cuddler who boldly unwrapped her wares five miles west of Erick, Oklahoma, Billie wiggled her way completely into her community's heart—and soul.

"When I started, locals were less than friendly," Billie admits. "But I'm a churchgoer. And I went to church. Pretty soon, I had my whole congregation working at my place."

The miracle that became Reptile Village began buckle square in the nation's Bible Belt. Billie Henderson hailed from Iowa. She and husband Grafton were simple carnival folk—concessionaires who traveled extensively and brokered games of chance. They specialized in the ring toss, and they traveled as far west as Lynnwood, Washington, to make their take of coins. But Grafton—nicknamed Grabbo—longed to give up gaming-booth life. As a younger man—and while working a midway in Georgia—he had developed a taste for exhibiting reptiles. Grafton dreamed of owning a stationery zoo. In 1964, he and Billie settled on Route 66 five miles west of Erick, Oklahoma. They began raising buildings they hoped would stand hypnotically still.

"One week after we opened, a tornado blew down all our buildings," Billie remembers. "But we rebuilt in 1965. We called our place Reptile Village."

Reptile Village was conceived and realized as a complete menagerie. Although named for and featuring things wiggling, Reptile Village housed a healthy share of warm-blooded mammals. Buffaloes, monkeys and fox roamed pens across a zoo that eventually boasted 22 cages.

Grafton and Billie bought beastly babies from local suppliers. Rattlesnakes and exotic reptiles were shipped by train into New Braunfels, Texas, from whence Grafton retrieved them by automobile.

"My husband went with Grafton to pick up the alligator," says one-time Reptile Village manager Rosalee Admire with a lingering edge in her voice. "They brought it back in a box. I can tell you, they got that alligator here just fine. But I'm not going to talk about the shape the two of them were in when they got back."

Grafton and Billie designed Reptile Village to comfortably wrap families in its coils. Accordingly, couples bringing kids to Reptile Village enjoyed significant discounts on the price of admission. A watermelon stand stuffed sweet little mouths with fruit, cider and flavored ice. Picnic tables sat under shade trees. Outdoor games—including an old standard ring toss—welcomed any tots wishing to try their luck.

Reptile Village suffered significantly few problems with its animals. The only enduring trouble occurred when tourists persisted in poking fingers into the monkey cage—and the monkeys persisted in biting them. Over and again, Billie drove nipped fingers to the doctor in Erick. She could imagine no situation more frustrating until the day Grafton unexpectedly died, and she was left to run Reptile Village alone.

"I couldn't find anyone to help me," Billie recalls of her first days as a reptile widow. "So I went to the church that I belonged to—the Church of Christ. I told them that I needed help. At one time or another, everyone from that church worked for me. I had six parishioners that worked at Reptile Village full time, and I had 15 or 20 that would come in whenever I called them. For a couple of years, the preacher himself cleaned the animal cages."

By the strangest turn of the worm, religious fundamentalists had joined forces with outright snakes. Abstainers who would never gamble came to Reptile Village to man its games of chance. Choral singers toiled in the curio store—showing state plates, spoons and ashtrays to an increasingly more fascinated crowd.

"I never had real turquoise jewelry—just imitation," says Billie. "And we *told* people it was imitation. I sold lots of steer horns every day. The dealers bought these raw horns in Galveston. They'd sell them to all the curio shops. They'd come by with their truck, and I'd buy all the horns they had for practically nothing. I had so many steer horns, I stored them in my cellar. I'd take customers from the front down to the cellar to look at the steer horns."

Righteous workers were on occasion unprepared for the caliber of customer that hopped in off the highway. As the Age of Aquarius dawned, hair grew longer—and so did the nerve of Reptile Village visitors. No one thought anything unusual about the Reptile Village burro that brayed happily every time it spied a man with long hair. Not until the day Billie stopped—and smelled illegal posies.

"That was in the hippie days," says Billie. "The hippies all loved animals, and the animals all loved the hippies. I had a burro in a pen outside the curio store. And whenever the hippies walked out the door of the curio store, that burro would start braying at them.

"I finally figured out what was going on. All the hippies were giving that burro a little pot, and he liked that. *That's* why he loved hippies so much!"

"The hippies would buy animals, too," adds Rosalee Admire. "They'd even buy baby coyotes and take them home and train them like dogs. We sold a lot of baby skunks in those days. Of course, we had the skunks defrosted."

Care of the Reptile Village marquee snake pit fell to Rosalee Admire. The state-of-the-art edifice was fashioned of concrete and filled with sand from the banks of a nearby river. The 25 to 30 diamondbacks inside enjoyed heat lamps during cold months, but cleanliness—while next to godliness—was still achieved by old-fashioned scrubbing. "Do you want to know how to clean a snake pit?" Rosalee asks. "You pull all the snakes to one side and get down there and scrub with bleach. Now, that's a fact."

One morning, Billie arrived at Reptile Village to learn that her buffalo had given birth. The pregnancy had gone undetected, and the calf's sudden appearance left everyone in awe. While workers gathered round to ponder the miracle, Billie called her sign painter and had the calf painted onto roadside billboards from Oklahoma City to Amarillo, Texas. The tiny-horned devil would become the biggest moneymaker Reptile Village ever had.

In time, the success of Reptile Village attracted envious eyes. Billie well remembers E. Mike Allred, a raccoon breeder and reptile handler who set up a snake shop between Erick and Sayre. The man who would take a leading hand in creating the famous Regal Reptile Ranch of Alanreed, Texas, made his stop near Erick short.

"He didn't know how to run his business," Billie bitterly maintains. "He just had snakes, and his place was very dirty. You never knew when or if he would open. We were the only two out there, but I would argue with him. He'd put signs for his business up in front of mine."

Billie Henderson stood her ground as Americans began shying away from roadside snake pits. She may be the only Route 66 reptile entrepreneur who advertised her business on TV. "I was on television for quite a while," Billie says. "That was in the days all television went off the air at 11 o'clock. I bought space on a radio station in Amarillo. I was on right behind Paul Harvey. As I made the money, I always put it back into the business."

In the middle 1970s, an interstate highway blew passed Billie Henderson and her Reptile Village. Unlike many owners of roadside establishments—who in the same situation elected to stay put and face dwindling returns—Billie packed her bags and left for sunnier ground. Today, she lives in Fontana, California. And while the remains of Reptile Village have crumbled and burned, Billie herself continues to confront life with the crisp determination of a tot tackling a ring toss. She remains plain spoken and rich with stories. An electric bundle of joy.

"I miss the people from my old congregation," Billie admits in quieter moments. "I'll always feel they were more reliable and more honest than other employees.

"Every time the calendar comes around to daylight savings time, I still call Rosalee. I still tell her to be sure and set her clock right. She or I always opened up Reptile Village. One of us was always early or late."

Out on the open road near Erick, Oklahoma, time, too, ticks along. And the rattler's wicked tail becomes a metronome marking time to days gone by. Strangely, the snaky psalm seems only half as sinister as it once seemed. But then, of course, the benediction is in. Faults have been forgiven, and everyone knows—in this day and age—there are many things more sinful than a roadside reptile house baring its teeth at passing cars and trying to snap up a measly 50 cents.

The truck owned by Billie Henderson's nemesis, E. Mike Allred, advertises the latter's Supernatural Raccoons. The truck now rests on the ranch of Ruth and Delbert Trew west of Alanreed, Texas.

Two of Addie Allred's pickled pets reside today inside the Devil's Rope Museum of McLean, Texas.

Mike's Menagerie & Reptile Garden, Cunningham's Neon Steer & Regal Reptile Ranch

Over the hiss of three hundred writhing bodies, the old woman blows up balloons.

The blueberry mark on her arm still burns, but she twists the rubber neck into another knot and chokes her feeble air into another finished product. Bites are simply part of her business. Occupational nibbles to be brushed with Bactine. Everyone suffered a nip now and then—even that teenager who sold her Texas diamond-backs by the bag.

Below, one of the hissing three hundred lunges after its lunch. Addie Allred looks downward to see the chick escaping—yellow chest heaving as it scrambles over mountains made of slinking, scaled shapes.

For a moment, Addie becomes a typical grandmother. Pity overwhelms, and she yearns to help the needy in this raging, wicked world. In the sweep of emotion, she picks up another dozen chicks—conveniently boxed like living cotton balls—and dumps them peeping helter-skelter into the poisoned hole.

Then the air cracks with leaping bodies, snakes pop like clock springs and death rains quickly in the stinging splat of venom. Addie Allred, above the brutal lunch, watches the carnage with a gentle, aging eye. She fastens a final balloon to the roof of the shed that houses her Den of Death and leaves it dangling like a brightly-colored meatball—another after-dinner toy for her well-fed, well-fanged wards.

More than any other enterprising pair, Addie and E. Mike Allred stand responsible for raising the snake pit to prominence on Route 66. A sister-brother team, they operated at least four slither houses during a reptile reign that lasted 30 years.

E. Mike's claim to fame stemmed from his ability to breed exotic raccoons. From the moment he opened Mike's Menagerie and Reptile Garden in Elk City, Oklahoma, he used his license to rear ring-tails as a stepping stone. E. Mike billed himself as "The Only Producer of the Most Colorful Raccoons in the World." He called his progeny "Supernatural Raccoons."

"The Supernatural Raccoons were raccoons with eyes that kinda glowed," says Delbert Trew, a retired rancher who now looks after remnants of the Allred establishments that have wiggled their way into the Devil's Rope Museum of McLean, Texas. "Mike Allred—he was an old carny. He fed these particular raccoons something. They say it doesn't hurt the animal, but it kinda made 'em glow. If you fed 'em long enough, they'd be kinda like albinos."

Glowing or not, the Supernatural Raccoons couldn't halt progress. When Interstate 40 bypassed the slice of 66 on which Mike's Menagerie and Reptile Garden sat, E. Mike looked for a new beastly venue. For a time he settled in Erick, Oklahoma, offensively near Billie Henderson and her Reptile Village. Eventually, he moved his animals to Alanreed, Texas—and the home of his headstrong sister, Addie Allred.

"People ask me to describe Addie Allred," says Delbert Trew, "and I tell 'em the joke about the Devil coming down to earth and entering a church during service. First the preacher lights out, then the choir, then the whole congregation—everybody runs but one little old man sitting in the first pew. The Devil asks this fellow, 'Aren't you afraid of me?' And the fellow says, 'Why should I be? I been married to your sister for 50 years.'"

FIVE EXOTIC COLORFUL RACCOONS AND A GRAY

PHOTOGRAPHED AT

MIKE'S MENAGERIE & REPTILE GARDEN

ROUTE 2 - ELK CITY, OKLAHOMA 73644

E. MIKE ALLRED, Owner

BREEDERS OF THE

BIG, EXOTIC, GOLD PALOMINO RACCOON
That Breeds Color Consistently

THE ONLY PRODUCER OF
THE MOST COLORFUL RACCOONS IN THE WORLD

No. 768 Commercial Breeders License

Reg. Claim No. Form J, Claim J, JU-12051 and 12052
Washington, D.C.

Front and back of a postcard featuring E. Mike Allred's Supernatural Raccoons.

Soon after settling his menagerie in Alanreed, E. Mike and sister Addie began arguing over money. Their relationship grew so rocky that E. Mike packed a suitcase full of pit vipers and left to open another zoo. He settled five miles east of McLean, Texas, in an old service station let by local, Conald Cunningham. The building came complete with an unbeatable eye-catcher—a colossal neon steer's head created by Cunningham himself.

Conald Cunningham's family had come to Wheeler County from Altus, Oklahoma. They came in covered wagons, and they ranched in a day when Route 66 had yet to be imagined. When the highway was planned, Cunningham's relatives donated land for the road's right-of-way. His parents built and operated one of the county's first service stations. Conald followed them into the fueling business, adding a bit of flare with his renowned neon steer.

Cunningham designed the neon steer to stand atop his service station's canopy—a great, glowing head that hovered visible for miles. A 13-foot I-beam formed the steer's brow. At each end, three-quarter-inch piping arced into horns. From tip to tip, the steer measured nearly 25 feet. Conald traced the head in multi-colored neon—fiery red for the eyes, and blue for the nose. "Where the nostrils were, I put flashing blue neon," Cunningham says. "That made him look like he was snorting every little bit." Would-be cowboys and shutterbugs stopped nightly to admire the blazing Angus in the sky.

When E. Mike rented the station, Cunningham fashioned for him the RATTLESNAKES: EXIT NOW sign that still stands east of McLean. Cunningham thought it only proper he help his new lessee. He saw a softer side in the sour, arrogant snake man. "I'd gotten to know E. Mike when he moved his snakes from Oklahoma to Alanreed," Cunningham says. "He took several trips, and he moved them in a Volkswagen bus. About the time he'd get to where I was, he always had engine trouble. I'd get him going again—to be neighborly.

"E. Mike told me a little about his past. He told me he had run a kind of a cafe, and I suspect an illegal gambling joint, in Elk City. He took a shine to me. He wanted me to go into the snake business—take his business over as if I was his son."

Snake sign built by Conald Cunningham.

E. Mike acquired rattlesnakes at the Rattlesnake Round-up in Mangum, Oklahoma. After E. Mike moved east of McLean, Cunningham attended the round-up with him as official snake purchaser. Cunningham soon realized why E. Mike needed him so badly: Years earlier, the gruff old man had inadvertently caused a handler to be bit. Since that time, no dealer would talk with him. Among the round-up's weigh-ins and carnival booths, Cunningham also realized the snake life was not for him. "The whole time they had people slaughtering snakes and frying 'em," he says with lingering distaste. "Rattlesnakes look like onion rings fried."

In July of 1979, E. Mike suffered a fatal heart attack while tending his snake attraction east of McLean. Cunningham's old gas station—minus the Neon Steer—eventually moved into McLean proper. Today it survives on the westbound lanes out of town as the Red River Steak House.

Mike's Menagerie and Reptile Garden rejoined its severed pieces back in Alanreed—as part of a snake house called Regal Reptile Ranch. E. Mike Allred faded from memory while his sister, Addie, became the unchallenged Queen of Panhandle Poison. Addie Allred, in fact, would steer Regal Reptile Ranch into the 1980's as the last substantial snake show on all of Route 66.

"Addie was the sweetest lady you ever wanted to meet," says Michael Bybee, a McLean native who worked at the ranch as a teenager. "After E. Mike died, I moved all the snakes for her from his place east of McLean to Alanreed. I took them in my '70 Chevelle. You couldn't hear the car radio over their rattling. On the way, I stopped at a Dairy Queen where my mom was working. I pulled up at the drive-thru to order a Coke—and she couldn't hear me over the loudspeaker. My mom came to the window to see what the noise was. She saw what was in my car and panicked, and then the whole building freaked out. I had 300 rattlers in boxes, and I had the king cobra, and I had ahold of the old boa, but he was all over the whole car inside."

To a deeper degree than any other Route 66 snake salesman, Addie Allred managed to squeeze a lasting impression into the minds of those she met. A woman of average height with a tuft of mousy hair, Addie's one remarkable trait lay in her inability to fear anything with a forked tongue. Accounts abound in which Addie, ungloved, retrieved squirming cobras from the bowels of burlap sacks. Occasionally, the stories say, she suffered bites. None proved too deep or too venomous.

Under Addie's charge, the raspy population of Regal Reptile Ranch grew to include over 400 specimens. Lowly mammals—including a bobcat, two coyotes and E. Mike's aging Supernatural Raccoons—were consigned to outdoor cages. Visitors paid admission to enter the ranch's main building and view things cold-blooded. Between the pens and aquarium that held snakes, toads and lizards, giant centipedes and tarantulas rounded out goose bumps. A box marked "Baby Rattlers" sat innocently near the door. Brave peekers found this last bin filled not with infant adders but plastic toddler toys.

The last of the red-hot Route 66 snake houses—Addie Allred's Regal Reptile Ranch. Most of its pieces were absorbed from Mike's Menagerie and Reptile Garden—including its trademark tin cobra, commissioned by E. Mike from an Oklahoma welder.

The Den of Death kept its pets year round. In the winter, Addie covered the den so the snakes would not freeze. The rattlers drifted into a semi-hibernation.

Behind the main building, a metal shed housed the Den of Death—a corrugated metal cube roughly five feet wide by ten feet long. The Den of Death was filled six inches deep with Texas diamond-backs. Chicken chicks were consigned to the den by the box full. For fun, Addie threw in balloons.

"That was something to show off to customers," explains Michael Bybee. "The way a snake senses heat. Addie kept blown-up balloons hanging around the den. You'd take a balloon that had been hanging there at atmosphere temperature and throw it into the den, and those snakes would never move. Then you'd grab yourself a fresh balloon and blow it up and throw it in there and every one of those snakes would hit it before it ever got close."

Other educational opportunities abounded at Regal Reptile Ranch. When snakes breathed their last, Addie would go to a back closet where she stored dozens of glass jars. She'd select a jar and fill it with formaldehyde. Then she'd pickle the deadly departed inside it and set the jar in permanent state on a shelf. In time, the walls of Regal Reptile Ranch became a kind of macabre mausoleum, and visitors came as much for the corked creep show as they came for the living attractions.

Today, Interstate 40 has long amputated Alanreed. Regal Reptile Ranch lies bulldozed and buried. At the Devil's Rope Museum in nearby McLean, Delbert Trew sets a jar in visitor hands.

"Our son found this when he was pokin' 'round where the ranch was awhile back," says Trew. "Hard to believe there used to be walls full of 'em."

The jar is small and labeled "hognose." It seems almost quaint until one realizes the tiny specimen bobbing within is not only one of the last of Addie Allred's pickled pets but one of the last snakes left for viewing on Route 66. Of the thousands of rattlers, racers and asps, cobras, corn snakes or big boa constrictors, little remains but this one dwindled worm. The thought humbles and leads to thoughts of one's own mortality. And it's precisely at that moment that you realize this wee, wrinkled remnant has managed to manipulate you like the largest house of venom. And the preserved pink of its mouth seems to curl into one very cunning smile.

Beyond town—on either side of the interstate— the old highway squirms its head in and out of holes. And the Snake himself is on it, hitching a ride on a passing pickup, crawling to comfort in the back bed and, somehow, still getting the best of every deal.

Prairie Dog Town creator Forrest "Fist" Ansley with two of his town's furry tenants.

Prairie Dog Town

rairie dogs can't ride bicycles. Presumably, this cut out their cameo in *Butch Cassidy and the Sundance Kid*. Their absence from other great western films baffles. While Sam Peckinpah shoot-em-ups snub these squeaky extras, Sergio Leone outlaws never find fistfuls of prairie dogs in squares at high noon. Yet, in their day, prairie dogs infested the West, wiggling under its crust in unruly, wild bunches.

Throughout his fast life, Forrest "Fist" Ansley took notice of these overlooked rodents. Prairie dogs were present during the years Fist ran Ansley's Pig-Hip Restaurant—barking and begging a handout on Amarillo's west side. Prairie Dogs stood front-and-furry center years later when Fist sold the Pig-Hip, moved across the street and opened Ansley's Musical Pig Shop. On the whole, Fist noticed, prairie dogs had cleaner language than the customers who sidled-up to order his saucy pork sandwiches.

Not that Fist pooh-poohed good-natured name-calling. Born Forrest W., Fist signed his pet name to legal documents. His brothers called themselves Pig and Mad Thad. Fist's grandfather, B.T., started the name game rolling when he led the Ansley family from Atlanta to Texas in the 1880s. B.T. ranched 17 years near Vernon before settling in Dumas above what became the Alibates Flint Quarries National Monument. Grandson Fist spent childhood years there, chasing prairie dogs and digging nuggets from the same ground that had supplied Indians with arrowheads. As Fist grew to manhood, Rockhound became another name to which he would answer.

Fist's father, B. T. Jr., was a land dealer who sold three million acres of the XIT Ranch, and moved to Amarillo to watch his sons wind their lives around the highway. Second-born Fist forged a career in the restaurant business, but when World War II struck, he found carhops in scant supply. Fist sold his business and went to Alaska on a fishing trip that lasted two years. When he returned to Amarillo, he became an innkeeper—buying the downtown Bungalow Courts with partners.

In the after-war years, Fist realized Amarillo's future depended on its ability to attract tourists. Route 66 daily pumped droves of travelers through the city. Fist believed highway betterment—and the right regional attractions—would make guests pause. In October of 1950, Fist became the president of a fledgling National U.S. Highway 66 Association. He served his term through 1951, dealing with such problems as Arizona's Oatman Bottleneck and the Bushland Deathtrap in his own state.

In January of 1952, Fist wrote to the *Amarillo Daily News*. He suggested someone build a guest ranch outside Amarillo and lay a road from the ranch to Boys Town. Cow camps, Fist explained, could be erected along the route and filled with photogenic cowboys. Tourists could drink coffee brewed over chip fires. The experience would mirror "the Old West with a vengeance." And the West, Fist insisted, was what visitors wanted from Amarillo.

In 1953, Fist became a director of the Amarillo Chamber of Commerce. He promoted Amarillo's Tourist of the Week campaign, a program that stopped a traveling family every seven days and showered them with free lodging, free dinner, free car service and gifts from local merchants. News clippings were as a matter of routine rushed to the lucky folks' hometown papers. But Fist remained convinced Amarillo should do more to offer travelers a taste of the true West.

"When Dad retired, he decided his hobbies were rocks and prairie dogs," says Fist's daughter, Jeanne McSwain. "He wanted to build a tourist attraction on Route 66. And so he built Prairie Dog Town."

Fist Ansley opened Prairie Dog Town in the spring of 1954. He designed it as a combination curio shop and zoo, and he built it around the varmint he believed best represented his region. At town's center sat the village itself, a quarter-block area that housed two colonies of prairie dogs. Fist was obliged to enclose the area in a fine wire mesh that stretched three feet above ground and four feet below to keep his tenants from escaping.

Tiny buildings filled the village at Prairie Dog Town. The hollow structures were made to look like banks and barber shops, stables and general stores. The village even boasted two outhouses and a Canadian River Dam. The prairie dogs instinctively dug holes under these odd-looking pieces of shelter. Visitors paid no admission to stand at village edge and watch the dogs acting neighborly.

"Inside Prairie Dog Town, there was a little building called Town Hall," says Jeanne McSwain. "And there was this old, scrubby-looking prairie dog with only one eye. He was evidently the patriarch of the village. When people came around, the other prairie dogs would scurry for their holes, but this old dog would climb atop Town Hall and defy everyone with his barking. So he was proclaimed the mayor of Prairie Dog Town." Fist fashioned a sign for the grand-standing rodent. He named him Bud Curtis— after Amarillo's then-current mayor.

Fist covered the inside of Prairie Dog Town's curio store with cattle horns. The collection included one set of sticklers that measured nine feet from tip to tip—donated by Fist's brother and horn dealer Paul "Pig" Ansley. Outside the store, Fist tethered two horses that children could ride. A live Texas longhorn and a chuck wagon stopped traffic. After the city of Amarillo outlawed large, living animals, Fist set up stuffed bucking broncs for photographers who wanted ponies in their pictures.

Prairie Dog Town was apparently populated by politically-aware pups: In 1954, the town's two "streets" were Eisenhower Boulevard and McCarthy Avenue.

Fist and daughter Jeanne inside Prairie Dog Town's curio store. The steer horns were placed by Fist's brother, Paul "Pig" Ansley.

Fist kept a few cages filled with prairie dogs in front of the curio store. These prairie dogs were personal pets—colony members abducted as babies and raised with human contact. Often, Fist strolled among customers with these friends on his shoulder. On occasion, Fist sold prairie dogs. He did a brisker business selling horned toads—loading the slow eaters into tiny boxes and shipping them as far as Japan. The toad market died when laws were enacted that stopped the lizards from leaving the state.

Fist never could gage how quickly his prairie dog population would grow. He knew only that an FHA housing project built behind Prairie Dog Town was overrun with escapees. Instinctively, prairie dogs did away with their young when colony numbers grew too large. However, no harm befell Moe and Smoe—a rare pair of prairie dog twins that became Prairie Dog Town marquee attractions.

As pups and profits of Prairie Dog Town grew, so did the schlock inside Fist's curio store. Among the store's best sellers were genuine cow chips that had been dried and varnished. Tourists reluctant to take true doo-doo home could buy ceramic cow pies painted with Prairie Dog Town's slogan: *This is the Country Where the Wind Pumps the Water and the Cattle Furnish the Fuel.*

"The salesmen pounced on Dad," says Jeanne McSwain. "One of the things they sent him was a set of salt and pepper shakers. They were in the form of a woman's breasts, and they said, 'Prairie Dog Town' across their front. When the next salesman came in, my mother said, 'I cannot stand this stuff!' The salesman said, 'If you hate it, order a gross. If you like it, order one or two.'"

Ever the faithful rockhound, Fist stocked souvenirs for fellow geology nuts. He filled bins with Alibates flint from the Ansley farm. The flint was fashioned into bookends, earrings and bolo ties.

In the early 1960s, Fist and his wife, Mabel, traveled to Australia's opal mines. They returned with an opal the size of an ostrich egg, and they displayed the opal at Prairie Dog Town. "Dad dug up skulls and arrowheads out in the family land," says Jeanne McSwain. "Even the little games that the Indian children would play. He displayed all of it in his curio store in what became a little museum."

Media types hounded Fist as a prairie dog expert. *World Book Encyclopedia* wrote its prairie dog entry with his help. *Life* magazine interviewed Fist for a series of nature books. With Prairie Dog Town established, Fist and Pig founded a curio store in an adobe building at Palo Duro Canyon. Pig placed a curio shop inside Homer Rice's Dining Salon. That store survives today at Amarillo's Big Texan Steak Ranch.

In the later 1960s, Fist Ansley truly retired. He had discovered that prairie dogs loved to chew mesquite roots, and ranchers were begging him to

Above: Prairie Dog Town's latter-day sign.

Below: Tourists consider a cactus while Fist's grandson Vance sells drinks.

bring the little buggers to clear their land of the bush. One day, Fist packed his prairie dogs, drove them into the country and released them en masse.

Prairie Dog Town's curio store in turn became a barbecue joint, a western store, a grocery and a liquor store. Fist dedicated his time to full-time rock-hounding. And Hollywood released *The Wild Bunch*, a Sam Peckinpah classic starring William Holden and Robert Ryan—and not one, single prairie dog.

"The prairie dogs are still there—on the grounds where Prairie Dog Town stood," assures Jeanne McSwain. "They probably always will be. That's just the way it is in the West. Once you have prairie dogs, you never get rid of them. You can try almost everything. They'll never go anywhere at all."

Everything short of getting them a Hollywood agent. And a haircut like Ernest Borgnine's.

Fist's granddaughter, Kate McSwain, feeds one of the town's tamer residents.

The put-upon horned toad—a rare player in any show of Mr. Lloyd's—was shown at Regal Reptile Ranch and sold at Reptile Village and Prairie Dog Town. "My children spent summers hunting the critters around Prairie Dog Town," says Jeanne McSwain. "They were paid 25 cents each for them. Fist either gave them away or charged a dollar for them. Most of the time they would put a soft piece of string or yarn around the toad's neck and put it in a little box. Hundreds of these horny toads were shipped all over the country and abroad."

Mr. Lloyd's Snake Pit

long the fast lanes of America's interstates, algebra and Einstein's theories find class dismissed. To enjoy our off-time stupidly seems the modern American Dream. Corporate-types too-long cooped want more than talky coffee breaks. Butchers, bakers and exhausted number-takers seek havens where no one raises a hand.

But on Route 66, and on Amarillo's west side, Kenneth R. Lloyd conducted curbside class. A traveling salesman for a farm supply company, Lloyd spent weekdays swerving up Texas backroads and slinging fertilizer and seeds. As he came upon snakes, he sacked the critters and stored them inside his trunk. When Lloyd returned to Amarillo, he'd place his new pets in a cinder-block pit that sat three-quarters of a mile east of the United States Helium Plant. There they became part of a slithering syllabus that tutored tourists for nearly ten years.

"Mr. Lloyd's Snake Pit was not a money-making thing," says anaconda aficionado, Bob Kerr. "Mr. Lloyd never intended it to be. The pit was a place where he could keep snakes that interested him. His entire emphasis was on education. He wanted people to see that snakes were not go-for-the-throat, rip-your-jugular-out sorts of animals."

Mr. Lloyd opened his pit in 1948. For roughly a decade, it remained an experiment in roadside unconformity. Mr. Lloyd's Snake Pit survived without benefit of souvenir store. No cider stand sold soft drinks. No gas pumps pushed pricey petrol. A small wishing well—stocked with spare rattlers—collected the equivalent of milk money. No one collected admission; no one took apples at the door. A makeshift sign positioned near the highway was the only public indication the pit existed.

Lloyd's workers were themselves venom fanatics who held other jobs. Bob Kerr came to work at Mr. Lloyd's Snake Pit during his teenage years. He was one of a handful of volunteers who took turns walking the pit and answering visitor questions.

Bob had discovered his scaly interest the day a snake handler visited his high school. "All my life I'd been told snakes were terrible animals—to avoid 'em and kill 'em," he remembers. "All of a sudden, this guy had seven boxes of snakes on the stage, and nobody died."

Bob Kerr was consuming books by pioneer herpetologists when he met a man named Ted Klein. Klein had connections to the San Antonio Zoo. He maintained a snake exhibit at Palo Duro Canyon, and he began permitting Bob to help him show snakes there. Among Klein's associates was another asp man—a fellow who sold fertilizer and approached the Snake on affectionate, textbook terms. His name was Kenneth R. Lloyd.

"Ted was very much into the spectacular, 'spooking-people' approach," Bob says. "When Mr. Lloyd picked up a snake, he tried to convince people that snakes were animals you could live around without fearing. His whole purpose was in trying to get people to accept snakes to some degree."

Bob Kerr became a regular at Mr. Lloyd's Snake Pit. He found the farm supply salesman who socked away snakes went out of his way to acquire new breeds. Lloyd had befriended the curator of reptiles at the San Antonio Zoo. He often met the man to swap Panhandle snakes for serpents of lower Texas.

"Mr. Lloyd had located a number of rattlesnake dens," Bob says. "In the spring, we'd catch specimens for the summer season. The best den Mr. Lloyd found was a ravine that had been filled in by the highway department. The fill was nothing but rocks stacked 20 feet high. We'd start at the bottom and move up the incline. We caught 87 rattlers in five hours, and it was pretty risky. Once you started up the face you had to keep moving, because rattlers came out of holes behind you."

Kenneth Lloyd attempted to feed his snakes a natural diet. He set live traps to catch native field mice and pooh-poohed boxes of farm-bought chicks. The balloon trick—presented on a routine basis at Regal Reptile Ranch of Alanreed, Texas—was used at Lloyd's Snake Pit only to silence hecklers who said Lloyd's snakes had been de-fanged. Workers milked venom from fangs, but only to illustrate how the job could be completed in reasonable safety.

"We tried very hard not to frighten anyone," Bob Kerr emphasizes. "One of the things we did to show that snakes were no tremendous risk to people was reach out with our hook and cover our feet with rattlesnakes while we lectured inside the pit. We explained to people, 'We're not moving, so the snakes don't know we're not a stump or a tree.' The whole time, onlookers couldn't see our shoes."

Snake handlers themselves learned lessons while working at Mr. Lloyd's. Bob Kerr remembers the day a six-foot western diamondback taught him a lesson in patience. The whopper had been in the pit less than two weeks when Kerr clumsily trod on its tail. Braced for a bite, he watched the snake stoically crawl away—adapted already to its new captivity. Conversely, Bob learned prairie rattlers never tamed. After years in Mr. Lloyd's Snake Pit, they reared and rattled at every approach.

"I'm not trying to look like a he-man," Bob assures, "but a bull snake popped me pretty good. I went to the animal shelter to pick it up. They had it in a cage. I reached in to pull it out, and it grabbed my hand between the thumb and forefinger. When a snake like that bites, you don't jerk because you worsen the bite; you can tear out his teeth, and the snake can get infected and die from that wound. I was at the animal shelter at noon. The only other person there was a jail trustee, and he was scared to death of snakes. He kept saying, 'He's going to eat you! He's going to eat you!' I said, 'No, but it's going to take him a little while to figure out he can't

eat me.' After awhile, the snake started working his teeth loose. When he released, I had a perfect impression of his teeth on my hand. The trustee screamed, 'You're going to die! You're going to die!' I said, 'No, I'm not. Hand me a paper towel.'"

In September of each year, Mr. Lloyd took a snake exhibit to the Tri-State Fair. Mr. Lloyd was at his best on these occasions, thrilled to bring his message to so many spectators at once. Inside a tent and around a temporary pit, alligators, turtles and gila monsters joined Lloyd's menagerie, borrowed for the fair's sake from the San Antonio Zoo.

Mr. Lloyd's Snake Pit disappeared from Route 66 after divorce struck the Lloyd home. Lloyd took his fanged friends and moved to Fritch, Texas. There he fashioned a snake exhibit on the town's main street. A lack of traffic soon shut it down.

Bob Kerr took his experience at Mr. Lloyd's Snake Pit and turned it into 47 years of educational snake talks to youth and civic groups. As later life took Kerr traveling, he stopped to examine other snake exhibits along Route 66. Kerr has his own theory on the demise of the roadside snake pit.

"A lot of the snake exhibits were short-lived to begin with," Kerr says. "Most of 'em were between Amarillo and Oklahoma City, and they'd be open for a year or so or maybe a summer. Many weren't well-stocked, and few attempted to give the tourist any kind of information about what they were seeing. I think when most tourists stopped at a snake exhibit, they felt they paid too much for what little entertainment they got. As a result, snake exhibits were not economically viable.

"Because Mr. Lloyd was bankrolling his own show, he turned his snake pit into something else. He *taught* people. And that was different. I've never been able to find out what happened to Mr. Lloyd. I'd sure like to let him know he's been an important person in my life."

Throughout the corridors that are America's interstates, the recess bell still rings. Vacationers stampede like flunking cattle, chewing postcards, snapping polaroids and jumping over a fast and frenzied moon.

At least, on Route 66, we've had opportunities to slow down and learn something.

Intermission: Cadillac Ranch & the Dynamite Museum

Sooner or Later, Everyone Goes to the Zoo.
—Dynamite Museum sign

rive-in aficionados well remember the cartoon commonly screened between an evening's first and second feature. While floodlights flared and burned bug-eyed over the path to the concession stand, animated treats performed circus tricks across the silver screen. The movie-night commercial wanted nothing more than to nudge nibblers into action. But nine times out of ten, we snackers stayed put and made our run for Raisinettes after the cartoon finished. We thought that somersaulting frank a keener hot dog than Mary Lou Retton. Intermission became an attraction in itself.

In the same manner, roadside amusements along Route 66 often became main attractions. Puttering toward the Ozarks or the Petrified Forest, every Route 66 traveler heard the call of a Buffalo Ranch or a Whoopee Coaster. Popular opinion called these establishments street-side intermissions—places at

The Cadillac Ranch—perhaps the most widely recognized roadside attraction in America today.

which to peek and get gone. But those of us brave enough to face the wagging finger of the National Park Service might confess we remember—and enjoyed—E. Mike Allred's Supernatural Raccoons as much as we enjoyed the Grand Canyon. The roadside attractions of Route 66 delighted first because they surprised. They stand bright in our memories because they had the courage to show us things more personable, less polished and often substantially stranger than our mainstream destinations.

In a wheat field west of Amarillo, Texas, the Cadillac Ranch reaps its share of arched eyebrows. An assembly line of coupes and sedans stabbed nose-down in the ground, the shrine to Motor City madness may be the most celebrated roadside attraction in today's United States. To date, the ten little orphaned autos have made the cover of *MAD Magazine*, the maps of Rand McNally, and the A-sides of Bruce Springstien singles. Those who know the ranch's preposterous papa speak with wonder of a wild-mannered Amarillo millionaire named Stanley Marsh 3.

Stanley, in fact, could be called the reigning King of Roadside Attractions. With the Cadillac Ranch—and his lesser-known Dynamite Museum—Stanley has turned Amarillo into ground zero for quirky, curbside sights. Exactly where Stanley's eye-popping projects will lead this old cowtown remains anyone's guess. Certainty says only that Amarillo today exudes more of the spirit of classic Route 66 attractions than any other city on America's favorite highway. And that is neither a small nor a mundane accomplishment.

One approaches Stanley Marsh 3 like a queasy centurion confronting the Emperor Caligula. Precisely, with silly hat in hands and a sinking suspicion your vital organs are about to be removed with an egg beater. Stanley remains one of the wealthiest and most influential men in the Texas Panhandle. A ranching and broadcasting baron, he keeps court in Amarillo's tallest tower—a glass and steel breadstick accessed via rocketing elevator ride. Passengers arriving on the umpteenth floor find silence beyond the sounds of their own surprise, startled by the sight of a dead body lying pretty and pink on the floor.

"That was Artemis," confides the lackey who comes to quiet your screams.

Artemis?

"Stanley's flying pet pig."

A squat and a scrutiny proves the toady speaks true: The blushing bump on the carpet *is* a deceased pig—and one that seems to have soared to the troughs of hog heaven wearing angelic green wings. The inky extras were tattooed on Artemis' port and starboard at Stanley's behest when the porker was quite young and alive. If quirkiness holds key to understanding roadside appeal, inquiring minds appear to have parked in the right place.

The dead piggy-turned-parrot is only the first non sequitur in Mr. Marsh's menagerie. The mortal remains of Artemis lie in the center of Stanley's Croquet Court—a room in which wickets had been stabbed into the floor to allow for the whacking of little gamy balls. There exists a thick smell of sideshow here, as if this room has sashayed back in time and into the prodigious gene pool that gave birth to P.T. Barnum's American Museum. There's a barber's chair, a crepe-paper elephant's head, a pink parking meter left by Rita and a hump of deformed metal that might once have been a real car. A strange, staring creature called a Pac-Man frog squats behind glass and eats.

"We fed him some mice yesterday," says Stanley Marsh 3, appearing as slickly as a genie from a Crisco bottle. "Someday he'll be able to eat a whole guinea pig."

Preconceived notions explode the moment Stanley Marsh 3 arrives on the scene. To meet Stanley is to meet no millionaire madman but a cattle-fed and gentle-mannered giant. With his Fuller Brush moustache and shaggy locks, Stanley seems the sort of fellow one finds on television espousing the goodness of oatmeal. Casual observation reveals little else—except that Stanley is apparently a well-read man. Even as he shakes hands, Stanley sets aside a book by Kurt Vonnegut, Jr., and lobs an allusion to *Huckleberry Finn* into the air. Astute guests do well to pull out their literary badminton rackets and swat back: Mr. Marsh's is a world in which one needs keep an eye on the intellectual birdie.

Stanley discusses All Things Creative in the dining space of his office. There, in a corner riddled white by buck-toothed windows, he entertains visitors while he lunches with his staff. The table at which all eat is inviting in its bigness—a launching pad over which hatters might gut watches, Egyptians embalm friends or Frankensteins fiddle with brains gone soft. Stanley, in his merry, metaphorical way, manages all of these tasks before passing the pickles.

"A long, long time ago, the Indian's lucky sign was three straight lines," Stanley offers in calm, hypnotic tones. "Straight lines represented value—arrows and tent poles. As the white man came with their dreaded rifles that shot straight, bars on their jails that locked you up, railroad tracks that went lickety-split and highways, the Indian began to realize he lived in a land of arcs. Straight lines became the devil's tools. And that's why we all get to be here in an upright, geometrically-built building with air conditioners and elevators."

History, for Stanley Marsh 3, seems a matter of minding details. His Route 66 is a running tally of Steinbeck's words, Mastersons named Bat and pieces of Amarillo architecture that he gleefully picks out from his window in the clouds. Stanley adores the old highway; of this, there can be no doubt. He finds in its lanes a freedom made fashionable by the All-American Automobile and a liberation experienced by puttering to points distant. Stanley's sense of wanderlust—and his adoration of art—led him to sponsor his most famous roadside attraction—the Cadillac Ranch.

Speaking specifically of the ten Cadillacs, Stanley alternately blows hot and evasive. Stanley will tell you the Cadillac Ranch is the best roadside attraction in the vicinity. He'll tell you the corroding collage was placed in 1974 by a San Francisco art commune called the Ant Farm. But eagle ears may detect the smallest hint of fatigue in Stanley's endorsements. The story of the Cadillac Ranch is a story many times told. For Stanley, the public's familiarity with the Cadillac Ranch saps the monument of part of its punch. "My theory is that it's better to see than be told about," Stanley states and sends the Curious George off to consider his latest roadside love—the Dynamite Museum.

When all is written in the annals of Texas history, the Dynamite Museum may well be recorded as the only institution without physical walls. A runaway concept with membership, the Dynamite Museum's primary activity involves sneaking diamond-shaped road signs into Amarillo yards, setting them in cement and leaving them for citizens to find. Unless landowners complain, each sign becomes part of a population overtaking Amarillo.

The signs themselves are painted by individual artists. Many carry famous quotes. Others sport catch-of-the-day jabberwock. On Tyler, along the western approach into town, a series of signs sings the praises of a personified fellow named ART. Signs share snippets from Marlowe and Wordsworth and chunks of *Kubla Khan* and *Julius Caesar*. There are detailed paintings of parrots, ponies and pigs on the beach, the notification "We've Confiscated Your Water Pistol" and the question "What Is a Village without Village Idiots?" "Men Like Snails, Men Like Eels, Men Like Slugs;" "Your Turn to Curtsy, My Turn to Bow" and "Sooner or Later, Everyone Goes to the Zoo" prime imaginations for the nursery rhyme at 4th and Louisiana:

Twinkle, twinkle, Little Lamb
Someone dipped you in mint jam.

Aesthetically, the Dynamite Museum evokes long-gone days before the enactment of the Ladybird Johnson Act when billboards ruled Route 66. Hand-painted letters hawked fantastic beasts like The Donkey With the Human Head and the 300-Pound Canary. Horizons were circus-colored, and the road-side attraction hit its stride making riders wonder what surprises lurked ahead. The true beauty of the Dynamite Museum lies not with its individual pieces, but with its ability to rekindle this type of traveling anticipation. No matter how many folks fire off Instamatics here, the signs of the Dynamite Museum can never become predictable. There are simply too many signs for anyone to effectively map or memorize. Through these outlandish portraits, these words of wit and colorful claims, Amarillo's streets become a recreation of what Route 66 once was—before every nook and cranny of the highway

This page: Grace and gobbledygook. The signs of the Dynamite Museum cover Amarillo in an artistic alphabet soup.

Bottom right: Stanley Marsh 3, in an Alfred Hitchcock mood, strolls in stark white through an Amarillo field.

became AAA-mapped Interstate, and the surviving sights were charted, alphabetized and awarded one to four sterilizing stars.

"The last quote I heard, the Dynamite Museum had erected 2800 signs," says David Trew, the interpreter who earlier explained the piggy remains of Artemis in Stanley's Croquet Court and now introduces you to Cinderella, a sow with six feet. Cinderella and her litter of piglets share space at Toad Hall—Stanley's Amarillo home. Nearby, peacocks pick around snod grass. A Volkswagen Slug Bug lies half-buried in the ground.

"You never know what to believe when it comes to Stanley," David Trew says of Amarillo's ongoing show. "I once heard he released a donkey in the halls of his high school. Another time, I heard he went into a pet store and released all the birds from their cages.

"But I do agree with Stanley when he says, if you can afford it, life should be like a circus. Most people walk around their humdrum lives, drive back and forth to work and take care of the kids, but they don't have any adventure."

Back in his office near Amarillo's ceiling, Stanley Marsh 3 picks up this thread, ready at last to openly discuss roadside attractions. "When I was a boy, you went up to everybody's dad and asked them, 'What do you do?' Now we have these places bigger than football fields where everybody does the same thing.

"Big chains and things decrease individuality," Stanley continues. "If I were King, I would outlaw big. I might outlaw franchising or mandate franchises do their own architecture or playgrounds. If I outlawed big, I don't know if there would be more places you'd call roadside attractions, but there would be more places to see that were different.

"Big is less happy."

At the end of his artful day, Stanley Marsh 3 appears to do what he does simply because it tickles him. Critics leave him unruffled. If the best-laid plans of mice and millionaires occasionally amount to diddley-squat, Stanley remains unconcerned. All that seems to matter to Stanley is the moment's viability. And the opportunity to dream in the road-side Dreamland that he claims to trip nightly wearing rabbit pajamas—where folks who die before they wake are chicken-fried like a steak.

The roadside attraction—as it lived and thrived on Route 66—was something unique, something unexpected and something often artful. The roadside attractions of Stanley Marsh 3 incorporate these characteristics while recognizing the ringmaster is always part of the show. Like P. T. Barnum—the first purveyor of modern amusement—Stanley Marsh 3 knows all is a matter of perspective. Just as Route 66 itself—in so many minds—remains more than a collection of secondary roads and overgrown stretches of asphalt, roadside attractions are what you make of them.

"The moon is my favorite work of art," Stanley says as the day's dusky curtains begin to drop. "You're too young to remember, but we made the moon when you were little. We built a catapult in the backyard—the kind used to knock down medieval castles—and we loaded the moon into it, and flung it up there. I've always been a little partial. Since we hung the moon."

Back at the Cadillac Ranch, the wind turns trunks into slide whistles. Cameras click, and an occasional face lingers to ask "What possessed the person who put these here?"

Few guess the answer floats back in Amarillo's brightly-painted guts—alone in a field near Wild Horse Lake. There, one sign of the Dynamite Museum stands apart from the others. With sharp, black letters carved over dull yellow, it could pass for a genuine road sign, if not for the message that rides like the cavalry after every rearview mirror—and trots as a tribute to all the old ringmasters who raised empires of amusement along old Route 66:

ALIVE

Albro, Aleene Kay. Papers. In possession of Betty Wheatley, Grove, Okla.

Argo, Burnis. "Bathhouse Use Revives In Claremore." *Daily Oklahoman,* 27 Jan. 1986.

"Bath Industry Began With Hunt for Heat." *Claremore (Okla.) Daily Progress,* 28 June 1953.

Barnett, Hayward. *Crystal Cave.* N.p., 1988.

Benedetti, Rose Marie. *A Village on the River, 1888–1988: A History of Lyons, Illinois, in Celebration of Its Incorporation.* Lyons, Ill.: Lyons Centennial Commission, 1988.

Benedetti, Rose Marie, and Virginia C. Bulat. *Portage, Pioneers and Pubs: A History of Lyons, Illinois.* Chicago: Angel Guardian Orphanage Press, 1963.

Bogdan, Robert. *Freak Show: Presenting Human Oddities for Amusement and Profit.* Chicago: Univ. of Chicago Press, 1988.

Bunyan, Clytie. "Theme Park Crossing New Frontiers." *Daily Oklahoman,* 26 April 1998.

Charton, Scott. "Jesse James to Rest in Peace—Again." *Associated Press,* 28 Oct. 1995.

Childers, Elbert and John F. Bradbury. "Basketville: Roadside Community on Route 66." *Newsletter of the Phelps County (Mo.) Historical Society,* n.s., 13 (April 1996).

Churnovic, Carrie. "The Price Is Right: Romeoville Flea Market Attracts Buyers, Sellers." *Joliet Herald–News,* 20 Aug. 1995.

Claremore, Oklahoma: The Home of Radium Water. N.p., Rogers County Historical Society, Claremore, Okla.

Clark, Marian. *The Route 66 Cookbook.* Tulsa: Council Oak Books, 1993.

Crawford, Jackie. "Wheatley, Dairy Ranch Still Going Strong After 38 Years." *Miami (Okla.) News–Herald,* 20 June 1997.

Crets, Jennifer Ann. "Water of Diamond Transparency: The Legacy of Chain of Rocks Waterworks Park." *Gateway Heritage,* vol. 15 (summer 1994).

"Crystal City Adds a 'Vacuum Cleaner,' Builds Water Plant." *Tulsa Tribune,* 6 July 1948.

"Crystal City Excitement a Memory." *Tulsa World,* 9 May 1988.

"Crystal City Opening Set for Saturday." *Tulsa Tribune,* 22 May 1943.

Curry, Kerry. "Cars Make 2–Mile Trip to New Site." *Amarillo Globe–News,* 21 Aug. 1997.

Curtis, C.H. (Skip). *The Missouri Route 66 Tour Book.* Lake St. Louis: Curtis Enterprises, 1994.

"Davis Worried About Rattler That Bit Him." *Tulsa Tribune,* 27 June 1939.

DeFrange, Ann. "30 Years and Still Slinging: Frontier City Founders Recall Olden Days." *Daily Oklahoman,* 13 June 1988.

Defty, Sally Bixby. "Chain of Rocks Gives Final Prize—Itself." *St. Louis Post–Dispatch,* 13 July 1978.

Dingus, Anne. "Meanwhile, Back at the Cadillac Ranch." *Texas Monthly,* July 1994.

Donna, Modesto J. *The Braidwood Story, 1860–1957.* Geneology Collection. Fossil Ridge Public Library, Braidwood, Ill.

Etter, Jim. "Kachina Doll Fares Better Than Kaw-Liga." *Sunday Oklahoman,* 12 Jan. 1997.

"Flying Stunts Thrill Crowds at Air Circus." *Pontiac Leader,* 28 Sept. 1930.

"Frontier City Due Expansion." *Daily Oklahoman,* 23 Nov. 1958.

"Frontier City Grows." *Daily Oklahoman,* 23 Feb. 1958.

Geving, Henry G. and Andrea C. Geving. Affidavit. Lincoln (Ill.) Library, Sangamon Valley Collection, 26 Aug. 1973.

"Grand Opening Success for Stuckey's Shoppe." *Altamont (Ill.) News,* 8 Feb. 1962.

"The Great American Roadside." *Fortune,* Sept. 1934.

"Half Owners of Wax Museum File Suit Against Other Owner." *Springfield (Ill.) State Register,* 1 Feb. 1972.

"Here's Your Chariot, Girls." *Windsor Border Cities Star,* 23 Sept. 1931.

Hi, Neighbor. *St. Louis Community News,* 26 Jan. 1955.

Howard, Orville. "Polished Horns Reminders of Texas' Early 'First Settlers.'" *Amarillo Sunday News–Globe,* 8 Nov. 1959.

Hubbard, James W. "Dixieland Was a Dream Realized." Sapulpa Historical Society, Sapulpa, Ok.

Jones, Jenk Jr. "Once Proud Crystal City Shattered: Memories Grow Like Weeds." *Tulsa Tribune,* 10 Sept. 1955.

"Jury Awards $93,800 to Wax Figures Sculptor, Wife." *Springfield (Ill.) State Journal–Register,* 9 Feb. 1976.

Keel, Erin. "Marsh Turning Town into 'Freakville.'" *Amarillo Globe–News,* 28 June 1998.

Kelly, Judith. "Follow in Lincoln's Footsteps." *Springfield (Ill.) State Register,* 24 Aug. 1973.

"The Legacy of the Alfred Mann Family: Daughter of Ada's Former Fiancé Now Owns Crystal Cave." *Springfield (Mo.) Sunday News & Leader,* 12 Sept. 1971.

"Local Beach Lovers May Pass By Blue Whale: Former Tulsa Zoo Curator Owns Swimming Hole." *Catoosa Times-Herald,* 22 July 1981.

"Local Gator Ranch Brings Tourists Close to Nature." *Tulsa World,* 20 June 1968.

Martin, Linda. "Color Returning to Blue Whale." *Tulsa World,* 12 Dec. 1996.

Maue, August. *History of Will County, Illinois.* Vol. 2. Topeka-Indianapolis: Historical Publishing, 1928.

"May 1 Goal for Wax Museum Reopening." *Springfield (Ill.) State Journal–Register,* 17 Apr. 1977.

McCullough, Edo. *Good Old Coney Island.* New York: Charles Scribner's Sons, 1957.

McDaniel, Toby. "Working on 'Stiffs' Is All Part of this Wax Sculptor's Life." *Springfield (Ill.) State Journal–Register,* 11 Sept. 1971.

"A Message from Lacy's." Claremore Daily Progress, 28 June 1953.

"Mr. Faustman's Little World." *Omaha World–Herald,* 21 June 1959.

"Mr. Mullen's Ore-Nate Eyeful." *Oklahoma's Orbit,* 10 Nov. 1963.

"The New and the Old." *Springfield (Mo.) Sunday News & Leader,* 12 Sept. 1971

Peller, Michelle. "Frontier City Gunfighters Recall Early Days at Theme Park." *Edmond (Okla.) Evening Sun,* 28 June 1998.

"Prairie Dogs May Be Plains Ranchers' Second Best Friend." *Amarillo Sunday News–Globe,* 7 June 1959.

"Prairie Dog Town for the Tourists." *Amarillo Daily News,* 5 Dec. 1953.

Prather, Dannie. "The Lincoln Museum." *Kentucky Living,* July 1990.

"Relic of First World War to Legion Parade." *Aurora (Ill.) Beacon–News,* 24 Sept. 1933.

"The Rev. Russell T. Rauscher Heads Nation's Most Unique Mission." *Oklahoma Forth Magazine,* Sept. 1958.

Rhoades, Jeff. "Big Texan Dishes Up Newest Attraction: Fangs Under Glass." *Amarillo Globe–News,* 1 Nov. 1996.

Rittenhouse, Jack D. *A Guide Book to Highway 66 (a facsimile of the 1946 first edition).* Albuquerque: Univ. of New Mexico Press, 1989.

Rogers, Larry Dean. "Galloping Beyond the Frontier." *Oklahoma Today,* March–April 1998.

Rogers, Will. *Daily Telegrams: Volume III, Hoover Years, 1931–1933.* Claremore, Okla.: Will Rogers Heritage Trust, 1979.

Ross, Jim. *Oklahoma Route 66: The Cruiser's Companion.* Oklahoma City: Ghost Town Press, 1992.

Ross, Tamie. "Gunslinger Draws on Fond Memories." *Daily Oklahoman,* 6 June 1998.

Ross, Tamie. "Memories Ride Trail Back to Frontier City's Beginning." *Sunday Oklahoman,* 17 May 1998.

Rossiter, Phyllis. "A Dream Village on the Main Street of America." *Brairwood,* Mar. 1989.

"Route 66 Group Picks Ansley as National Chief." *Amarillo Sunday News,* 15 Oct. 1950.

Sanken, Barbara. "A Hard Road to Route 66." *Pontiac (Ill.) Daily Leader,* 11 June 1993.

Scott, Quinta, and Susan Croce Kelly. *Route 66: The Highway and Its People.* Norman: Univ. of Oklahoma Press, 1988.

"Seabourne Bros. in Parachute Acts at Local Airport." *Pontiac Leader,* 24 Oct. 1931.

Seloti, Joe. Papers. In possession of Dorothy Zaubi, Springfield, Ill.

Shepherd, Dave. "Pottowattomi, Gypsies Part of Lyons History." *Falcon,* 3 Mar. 1978.

Smith, Bill. "The Mule: Souvenir Shop Is Ozarks Institution." *St. Louis Post–Dispatch,* 21 May 1991.

Stephens, Bud. "Texas, Oklahoma Dedicate 66 as Will Rogers Highway." *Amarillo Daily News,* 27 June 1952.

Sterling, Robert E. *A Pictorial History of Will County.* Vol. 2. Joliet: Will County Historical Publication Co., 1976.

Stern, Elaine. "Death of an Amusement Park." *Profile St. Louis,* 8 Dec. 1977.

Swayzee, Cleon II. "The Bell Tolls for the Last of Area's Old-Fashioned Amusement Parks." *St. Louis Post–Dispatch,* 19 Sept. 1976.

Taylor, Janice. "End of an Era: Route 66 Landmark on Auction Block." *Miami (Okla.) News–Record,* 12 Oct. 1997.

"The Y—A Home Away from Home." *Amarillo Daily News,* 19 Jan. 1952.

Teague, Tom. *Searching for 66.* Springfield, Ill.: Samizdat House, 1991.

Wallis, Michael. *Route 66: The Mother Road.* New York. St. Martin's Press, 1990.

Weiss, John. *Traveling the New, Historic Route 66 of Illinois.* Frankfort, Ill.: A.O. Motivation Programs, 1997.

Weaver, H. Dwight. "A Brief Report on the Onyx Mining Industry of Missouri, 1890 to 1915." Missouri Department of Natural Resources' Division of Geology and Land Survey, August 1997.

Weaver, H. Dwight, and Paul Johnson. *Meramec Caverns in Legend and History.* Stanton, Mo.: H. Dwight Weaver and Paul Johnson for Meramec Caverns, 1995.

Witzel, Michael Karl. *Route 66 Remembered.* Osceola, Wis.: Motorbooks International, 1996.

"Wonders of the Chicago World's Fair." *Modern Mechanix and Inventions,* vol. 10. (Sept. 1933).

Woodcock, Lola, and George C. Woodcock. "Ozark Rock Curios: A Short History." In possession of Earl and Edie Woodcock, St. Clair, Mo.

The WPA Guide to 1930s Missouri. Lawrence, Kans.: Univ. Press of Kansas, 1986.

The WPA Guide to 1930s Oklahoma. Lawrence, Kans.: Univ. Press of Kansas, 1986.

Yirsa, Gladys. "Mini Histories of Lyons, Illinois." Lyons Public Library, Lyons, Ill., 1976.

"Young Normal Woman Killed in Parachute Jump." *Pontiac Leader,* 26 May 1930.

Younger, Willa. "Where Buffalo Roam: Oklahoma Trading Post Had Modest Beginning." *Joplin Globe,* 25 Jan. 1981.

Interviews & Acknowledgements

Donna and John Ackenhausen; Lloyd Adamski; *Amarillo Globe–News;* Rosalee Admire; Leo and Aleene Albro; Gwen Allen; Art Institute of Chicago; Herb and Jody Baden; Bobby Bell; Ben Bishop; Boots Motel; Hubert Boswell; John Bradbury; Buffalo Ranch; Mary "Betsy" Burton; Michael Bybee; Elbert Childers; *Claremore Daily Progress;* Guy Clevenger; Randy Clutter; Carolyn Comfort; Crystal Cave; Conald Cunningham; *Daily Oklahoman;* Zelta Davis; Davy Delgado; Devil's Rope Museum; Dixie Truckers Home; Luanda Doffer; Dynamite Museum; Dean Evans; Exotic Animal Paradise; Robert Faustman; John and Janie Ferguson; Bob Fish; Beryl Ford; Fossil Ridge Public Library; Tammy Franklin; Frontier City; Joy Galloway; Jim Gauer; Hank and Barbara Geving; John and Beverly Greer; Violet Grush; Jo Ann Haag; Darla Hall; Levi Harlin, Jr.; Dan Harlo; Betty Harris; Roy Heim; Billie Henderson; Rich and Linda Henry; Joe Howard; James Hubbard; Ariele Huff; Jesse James Wax Museum; Paul A. Johnson; Ralph Jones; Tim and Alice Jones; Kansas Grassroots Art Association, Inc.; Bob Kerr; Melba Knowles; Bob and Peggy Kraft; Shirley Lang; Rowena Lehman; Lincoln Library; Gerry Linhardt; Lyons Historical Society; Lyons Public Library; Curtis Mann; Stanley Marsh 3; Francis Marten; Lou Mavros; Karlene McAllister; Bob McCarty; Jerry McClanahan; J.E. McGuire; Jeanne McSwain; Meramec Caverns; *Miami News–Record;* Georgia Miller; Mike Mills; Missouri Department of Natural Resources; Missouri Historical Society; Missourian Publishing Company; Richard and Lisa Moffit (and their critters); Mule Trading Post; Jim Mullen; Ralph Mullen; Mullen's 66; Munger Moss Motel; Beth Nelson-Owen; Scott Nelson; Wanda Newton; Marjorie O'Brien; Kelley O'Bryan; Paula O'Bryan; Mary Ogg; Oklahoma Route 66 Association; Old Log Cabin; Old Route 66 Association of Texas; Old Town Museum; Glen Oldham; 100th Meridian Museum; Onondaga Cave State Park; Onyx Mountain Caverns; *Out West;* Tom Owen; Marvin Peters; Phelps County Historical Society; Plainsman Museum; *Pontiac Daily Leader;* Pontiac Historical Society; Barbra Pool; Wanda Queenan; Rebecca Ransom; Pat Reader; Chuck Reid; Loyd and Edith Richardson; Richard Risor; Charlotte Rittenhouse; the Riviera; Travis Roach; Jack Roberts; Naoma Robinson; Rogers County Historical Society; *Rolla Daily News;* Jim Ross; Route 66 Association of Illinois; Route 66 Association of Missouri; *Route 66 West;* St. Clair Historical Society; Sapulpa Historical Society; Barbara Sancken; Rick Sanders; Bernice Schoppe; Robert Sear; Mary Selotti; Emil Sergo; Gordon and Norma Sheplor; Deron Smith; Wayne Smith; Southwestern Tulsa Historical Society; Eugene Stanley; Louis Stastny; Tom Teague; Craig Thiltgen; Harry and Agnus Thiltgen; Carol Thole; Ralph Thole; Greg Thone; Pat Thone; Totem Pole Trading Post; Trailnet, Inc.; Brad and Deb Trainor; David Trew; Delbert and Ruth Trew; Judy Turilli; Les Turilli, Jr.; Jane Twing; Eugene Vale; Village of McCook; June Walker; Michael and Suzanne Wallis; H. Dwight Weaver; John and Lenore Weiss; Jim and Betty Wheatley; Jack and Janiece Whittman; Kathy Wilken; Will Rogers Center; Will Rogers Heritage Trust; Fletcher Williams; Chuck Woodbury; Earl and Edie Woodcock; Gladys Yirsa; Doris Yokam; Dorothy Zaubi

Special thanks to Curtis Osmun, a longtime friend and a patient traveling companion, who aided me with the final research for Fairyland Park, Montana Charlie's Little America, Rossi's Ballroom at Eagle Park, Ozark Rock Curios, Onondaga Cave, Crystal Cave and Radium Town. Special thanks also to Liz and J.P. Palmas for their willing ears and their unconditional support over the last seven years. And a bow to Ashley Bogle for her artistic integrity.

Above all, I thank my wife and lifelong traveling companion, Rebecca Repp, for her nine-to-midnight assistance on this project, her untiring field work, her unswerving faith in me and her shared belief that the roadside entrepreneurs of Route 66 deserved to see their stories told. If Route 66 is the Road of Wonders, she truly remains my miracle.

Photo Credits

viii: above, courtesy Lyons Historical Commission; below, author's collection
4: courtesy Georgia Miller
5: courtesy Lyons Historical Commission
6: courtesy Lyons Historical Commission
7: courtesy Georgia Miller
9: author, 1998
10: courtesy June Walker
12: courtesy June Walker
13: above, author, 1998; below, courtesy June Walker
14: courtesy Mary Ogg
16: courtesy Mary Ogg
17: courtesy Mary Ogg
18: courtesy Mary Ogg
19: courtesy Mary Ogg
20: author, 1997
21: author, 1997
22: courtesy Route 66 Association of Illinois
23: courtesy Route 66 Association of Illinois
25: above, author, 1997; below, author, 1998
26: courtesy Dorothy Zaubi
27: courtesy Dorothy Zaubi
28: courtesy Dorothy Zaubi
29: courtesy Dorothy Zaubi
30: author's collection
32: courtesy Hank Geving
33: courtesy Hank Geving
35: courtesy Sangamon Valley Collection, Lincoln Library
36: courtesy Hank Geving
38: courtesy Mike Mills
40: courtesy Mike Mills
41: courtesy Mike Mills
42: courtesy Pat Thone
44: courtesy St. Clair Historical Society
46: author, 1998
47: courtesy Earl and Edie Woodcock
50: courtesy Earl and Edie Woodcock
51: courtesy Earl and Edie Woodcock
52: courtesy Earl and Edie Woodcock
53: courtesy Earl and Edie Woodcock
55: author, 1997
56: author, 1997
57: courtesy Les Turilli, Jr.
59: courtesy H. Dwight Weaver
60: above, courtesy Les Turilli, Jr.; below, author, 1997
63: author, 1997
64: courtesy Missouri Department of Natural Resources
66: courtesy Missouri Department of Natural Resources
67: courtesy Missouri Department of Natural Resources
68: courtesy Missouri Department of Natural Resources
69: author, 1998
70: above, courtesy Rolla Daily News; below, author, 1997
71: courtesy Herb Baden
74: author, 1997
76: courtesy Tim Jones
77: courtesy Ralph Jones
78: courtesy Elbert Childers
79: courtesy Elbert Childers
80: author, 1997
82: courtesy Elbert Childers
83: courtesy Elbert Childers
84: courtesy Beth Nelson–Owen
87: author's collection
88: author, 1997
89: courtesy Exotic Animal Paradise
90: author, 1997

92: courtesy Loyd and Edith Richardson
94: courtesy Loyd and Edith Richardson
95: courtesy Loyd and Edith Richardson
96: courtesy Loyd and Edith Richardson
97: author, 1998
98: author, 1997
100: author, 1997
101: author, 1997
102: author, 1997
104: courtesy Betty Wheatley
106: courtesy Betty Wheatley
107: author, 1996
108: courtesy Betty Wheatley
109: courtesy Betty Wheatley
110: courtesy Betty Wheatley
111: author, 1996
112: courtesy Carolyn Comfort
113: courtesy Rogers County Historical Society
114: courtesy Joy Galloway
116: courtesy Rogers County Historical Society
117: author 1996
118: courtesy Claremore Daily Progress
120: courtesy Claremore Daily Progress
122: courtesy Rogers County Historical Society
123: author, 1998
124: author, 1996
125: courtesy Zelta Davis
126: courtesy Zelta Davis
127: courtesy Zelta Davis
128: courtesy Zelta Davis
129: courtesy Zelta Davis
130: courtesy Zelta Davis
131: author, 1997
132: courtesy Southwestern Tulsa Historical Society
135: courtesy Southwestern Tulsa Historical Society
136: courtesy Sapulpa Historical Society
137: courtesy Sapulpa Historical Society
138: courtesy Sapulpa Historical Society
139: courtesy Sapulpa Historical Society
140: courtesy The Oklahoma Publishing Company
142: author's collection
143: author's collection
144: courtesy The Oklahoma Publishing Company
145: author's collection
146: author, 1997
147: author, 1997
148: courtesy Wanda Queenan
149: courtesy Wanda Queenan
150: courtesy Wanda Queenan
151: courtesy Wanda Queenan
152: courtesy Collection of Jerry McClanahan
155: author, 1997
156: author, 1997
158: author's collection
159: author, 1997
160: courtesy Devil's Rope Museum
161: author, 1996
162: courtesy Jeanne McSwain
164: courtesy Jeanne McSwain
165: courtesy Jeanne McSwain
166: courtesy Jeanne McSwain
167: courtesy Jeanne McSwain
168: courtesy Moriarty Historical Museum
171: author, 1997
174: bottom right, courtesy Stanley Marsh 3; all others author, 1997
176: author, 1996
184: courtesy Zelta Davis

To Order Additional Copies of This Book:

Credit card orders in the United States call toll-free 1-877-285-5434.

Or send $34.95 plus $6.95 for shipping and handling to: Mock Turtle Press, Box 3168, Lynnwood, WA, 98046-3168.

Visit our website at www.mockturtlepress.com

Washington residents add 8.6% sales tax.